Other books by Janis Harsila, R.D. and Evie Hansen
**Seafood: A Collection of Heart-Healthy Recipes**

Other books co-authored by
Janis Harsila, R.D., or Evie Hansen
**Selling Seafood**
**Seafood Treasures**

Design and illustrations by Martine Richards Fabrizio
Typesetting and production by
Technigraphic Systems, Inc. — Edmonds, Washington
Editor — Diane Baker
Printing by Bookcrafters — Chelsea, Michigan
Cover photo — Alaska Seafood Marketing Institute

Special Thanks To:

National Fisheries Institute
Seafood Business
Mary Kay Sisson — Recipe Testing
Nutrition Works, Edmonds, Washington — Diabetic Exchanges

**PUBLISHED BY NATIONAL SEAFOOD EDUCATORS**

Light-Hearted
SEAFOOD
· TASTY · QUICK · HEALTHY ·

Janis Harsila, R.D. and Evie Hansen

National Seafood Educators
Richmond Beach, Washington

National Seafood Educators
P.O. Box 60006
Richmond Beach, WA 98160
(206) 546-6410

Printed and bound in the United States of America

First Edition

ISBN: 0-9616426-1-0

Library Of Congress Catalog Card Number: 89-90855

*Dedicated to David and Randy and
the commercial fishing industry.*

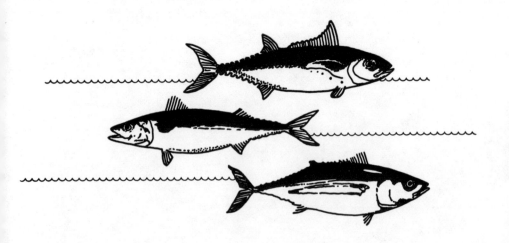

# TABLE OF CONTENTS

# Just About
# SEAFOOD

## CHAPTER 1
# JUST ABOUT SEAFOOD

# SEAFOOD: NATURALLY LIGHT

In 1984, the average consumer in the United States ate 13 pounds of seafood. By 1986 this amount had increased to 15 pounds of seafood per person. It is clear that people in the U.S. are eating more seafood. The health community has recognized seafood's benefits and seafood is now recommended as an integral part of a well-balanced diet by most major health organizations in the country. Most organizations suggest including seafood in our diets TWO TO FOUR TIMES PER WEEK.

**Seafood fits into a heart-healthy diet because it is:**
- low in calories;
- high in protein;
- low in total fat, saturated fat and cholesterol;
- high in polyunsaturated fats and omega-3 fatty acids;
- low in sodium;
- a good source of vitamins and minerals such as thiamin, riboflavin, pantothenic acid, niacin, phosphorus, potassium, iron, iodine, fluoride, zinc, selenium and copper;
- easily digested — great for children and the elderly!

## DICTIONARY OF SYMBOLS

 Hints or facts.

 Seafood on the Run — recipe preparation time: 15 to 20 minutes.

 Seafood is Kid Food — recipes that kids will love.

 Microwave recipes

**T.** Tablespoon

**tsp.** Teaspoon

**Nutritional Calculations:** When a range of servings is given, calculations are based on the larger serving size number. i.e. If there are 4-6 servings, the calculations are based upon 6 servings.

# OMEGA-3 FATTY ACIDS

New and exciting research in the last 20 years has shown seafood to have many health benefits. Omega-3 fatty acids play an important part in these benefits. Seafood contains high amounts of polyunsaturated fats and these fats contain significant amounts of omega-3 fatty acids. Omega-3 fatty acids are highly unsaturated fats, even more so than vegetable oils.

There is a very important reason why these unsaturated fatty acids are found in seafood: omega-3 fatty acids stay fluid at very cold temperatures and act as "anti-freeze" for seafood living in cold waters. *All* seafood contain omega-3 fatty acids, and those living in colder waters contain the largest amounts.

There are numerous studies currently being done on the effects of omega-3 fatty acids in the body and how much or how little omega-3 fatty acids we need to eat for maximum health benefit. Areas of research include: the beneficial effects of omega-3 fatty acids on heart disease and inflammatory diseases such as rheumatoid arthritis; omega-3 fatty acids possibly protecting the body from some cancers such as breast cancer in women; and omega-3 fatty acids possibly protecting the body from diabetes, high blood pressure, psoriasis, and migraine headaches.

Eating seafood with their omega-3 fatty acids may help us be healthier for life!

# CORONARY HEART DISEASE

The most publicized area of omega-3 fatty acid research at present is coronary heart disease. Omega-3 fatty acids seem to play a protective role in helping the body fight heart disease. Cholesterol and triglyceride levels can often be lowered by omega-3 fatty acids in the body. Of the two, triglycerides seem to be the most sensitive to omega-3 fatty acid intake.

By increasing seafood consumption, blood becomes thinner and is less likely to clot and form atherosclerotic plaques on blood vessel walls (hardening of the arteries). Omega-3 fatty acids also appear to affect blood HDL and LDL levels. HDL's (high-density lipoproteins) are the good guys in our blood. They remove used cholesterol from the body's tissues. HDL's are also believed to help ward off atherosclerosis. HDL levels appear to stay the same or increase by the consumption of more seafood.

LDL's (low-density lipoproteins) are the bad guys in our blood. They transport cholesterol from the liver throughout the bloodstream. LDL's are associated with the onset of atherosclerosis. LDL levels appear to decrease with increased seafood consumption.

SUMMARY OF
# DIETARY RECOMMENDATIONS
## OF MAJOR HEALTH ORGANIZATIONS

FROM: **American Heart Association**
**American Cancer Society**
**American Diabetes Association**
**Surgeon General's Report of Nutrition and Health — 1988**

Here are guidelines to achieve optimum nutritional health and to lower risk of diabetes, heart disease and cancer.

---

**All recipes in this book follow these dietary guidelines.**

---

## WELL-BALANCED DIET
- Meet your daily need for protein, vitamins and minerals.

## FATS AND CHOLESTEROL
- Reduce your total fat intake to 30% of your total calories.
- Limit foods containing saturated fat and cholesterol. Limit cholesterol to less than 300 mg per day.
- Substitute polyunsaturated and monounsaturated fats for saturated fat whenever possible.
  **Polyunsaturated Oils and Margarines,** listed here by polyunsaturated fat content (highest to lowest): safflower, sunflower, corn, partially hydrogenated soybean and cottonseed oil.
  **Monounsaturated oils:** olive and peanut oil.

## PROTEIN SOURCES
- Select small portions of low fat protein foods such as FISH AND SHELLFISH, lean meat, skinless poultry and legumes.
- Avoid salt-cured, smoked or nitrate-cured foods such as bacon, ham or hot dogs.
- Consume a maximum total of six ounces of protein foods daily (as recommended by the American Heart Association).

## DAIRY PRODUCTS
- Choose low fat dairy products such as skim milk, low fat cottage, Ricotta and Mozzarella cheeses.

## COMPLEX-CARBOHYDRATES AND INSOLUBLE FIBER

- Increase consumption of whole-grain foods and cereal products, vegetables (including dried beans and peas) and fruits.
- Eat more cabbage family vegetables such as broccoli, cauliflower, brussels sprouts, cabbages and kale.
- Choose more foods with vitamin A such as carrots, peaches, apricots, squash and broccoli.

## SOLUBLE FIBER

- Include three or four servings a day of foods high in soluble fiber, such as oatmeal and oat bran, apples, pears and citrus fruits, dried peas, beans and lentils as well as many vegetables, to help the body eliminate cholesterol.

## WEIGHT CONTROL

- Achieve and maintain your ideal body weight by controlling calorie intake and increasing energy expenditure through regular exercise.

## SODIUM

- Reduce intake of sodium by choosing foods relatively low in sodium.
- Limit the amount of salt added in food preparation and at the table to less than 1 teaspoon per day.

## ALCOHOL

- Use in moderation.
- Avoid drinking when pregnant.

## CIGARETTES

- Avoid cigarette smoking.

## PROFESSIONAL ADVICE

- Ask your doctor or nutritionist for specific advice before making major dietary changes.

# NUTRITIONAL BREAKDOWN OF FISH:

| 100 grams, 3½ oz. Raw, edible portion | *HF MF LF | Calories | Protein (grams) | Fat (grams) | Sodium (mgs) | Cholesterol (mgs) | Omega-3 fatty acids (grams) |
|---|---|---|---|---|---|---|---|
| Bass, freshwater | MF | 114 | 18.9 | 3.6 | 70 | 68 | 0.3 |
| Bluefish | MF | 124 | 20.0 | 4.2 | 60 | 59 | 1.2 |
| Catfish, Channel | MF | 116 | 18.2 | 4.3 | 63 | 58 | 0.3 |
| Cod, Atlantic | LF | 82 | 17.8 | 0.7 | 54 | 43 | 0.3 |
| Cod, Pacific | LF | 82 | 17.9 | 0.6 | 70 | 40 | 0.2 |
| Croaker | LF | 85 | 18.0 | 0.8 | 80 | 50 | 0.2 |
| Flounder | LF | 90 | 18.1 | 1.4 | 56 | 50 | 0.2 |
| Grouper | LF | 87 | 19.3 | 0.5 | 80 | 50 | 0.3 |
| Haddock | LF | 80 | 18.2 | 0.5 | 60 | 60 | 0.2 |
| Halibut | LF | 105 | 20.9 | 1.2 | 60 | 50 | 0.4 |
| Herring | HF | 150 | 18.3 | 8.5 | 75 | 80 | 1.7 |
| Hoki | LF | 74 | 15.7 | 0.8 | 109 | 30 | 0.3 |
| Lingcod | LF | 85 | 17.6 | 1.1 | 59 | 52 | 0.2 |
| Mackerel | HF | 160 | 21.9 | 7.3 | 80 | 40 | 2.5 |
| Mahi Mahi | LF | 102 | 21.0 | 1.0 | 130 | 85 | 0.1 |
| Monkfish | LF | 70 | 15.5 | 1.0 | 18 | 35 | N/A |
| Orange Roughy | LF | 65 | 14.7 | 0.3 | 63 | 58 | 0.1 |
| Perch, Ocean | LF | 95 | 19.0 | 1.5 | 70 | 60 | 0.2 |
| Pollock | LF | 85 | 19.5 | 0.8 | 60 | 50 | 0.5 |
| Pompano | HF | 164 | 18.5 | 9.8 | 65 | 50 | 0.6 |
| Rockfish (snapper) | LF | 97 | 18.9 | 1.8 | 50 | 40 | 0.5 |
| Sablefish (black cod) | HF | 130 | 17.9 | 5.7 | 55 | 65 | 1.5 |
| Salmon: | | | | | | | |
|   Chinook | HF | 180 | 20.0 | 10.4 | 45 | 66 | 1.4 |
|   Chum | MF | 120 | 20.0 | 3.8 | 50 | 74 | 0.6 |
|   Coho | MF | 146 | 21.6 | 5.6 | 46 | 39 | 0.8 |
|   Pink | MF | 116 | 19.9 | 3.5 | 67 | 52 | 1.0 |
|   Sockeye | MF | 168 | 21.3 | 8.6 | 47 | 62 | 1.2 |
|   Salmon, canned | MF | 160 | 21.8 | 8.0 | 420 | 62 | 1.2 |
| Sea Bass | LF | 97 | 18.4 | 2.0 | 68 | 41 | 0.6 |
| Shark | MF | 130 | 20.0 | 4.5 | 79 | 51 | 0.8 |
| Skate | LF | 95 | 20.0 | 1.0 | N/A | N/A | N/A |
| Smelt | MF | 97 | 17.6 | 2.4 | 60 | 70 | 0.7 |
| Sole | LF | 70 | 14.9 | 0.5 | 55 | 45 | 0.1 |
| Sturgeon | MF | 105 | 16.1 | 4.0 | 284 | N/A | 0.3 |
| Swordfish | MF | 120 | 19.4 | 4.4 | 70 | 50 | 0.2 |
| Tilefish | LF | 90 | 18.6 | 1.2 | 53 | N/A | 0.4 |
| Tuna, albacore | MF | 102 | 18.2 | 3.0 | 50 | 25 | 1.3 |
| Tuna, water-packed | LF | 130 | 29.6 | 0.5 | 356 | 20 | 0.1 |
| Trout, rainbow | HF | 195 | 21.5 | 11.4 | 52 | 50 | 0.5 |
| Whiting | LF | 95 | 21.3 | 1.2 | 50 | 20 | 0.4 |

# NUTRITIONAL BREAKDOWN OF SHELLFISH:

| 100 grams, 3½ oz. Raw, edible portion | *HF MF LF | Calories | Protein (grams) | Fat (grams) | Sodium (mgs) | Cholesterol (mgs) | Omega-3 fatty acids (grams) |
|---|---|---|---|---|---|---|---|
| **CRUSTACEANS** | | | | | | | |
| Crab, Alaskan | LF | 75 | 15.2 | 0.8 | 70 | 60 | 0.3 |
| Crab, Blue | LF | 87 | 18.0 | 1.1 | 293 | 78 | 0.3 |
| Crab, Dungeness | LF | 81 | 17.3 | 1.3 | 266 | 59 | 0.3 |
| Crab, imitation | LF | 90 | 13.4 | 0.1 | 600 | 50 | 0.2 |
| Lobster | LF | 90 | 16.9 | 1.7 | 210 | 85 | 0.2 |
| Shrimp | LF | 90 | 18.8 | 0.8 | 140 | 158 | 0.3 |
| **MOLLUSKS** | | | | | | | |
| Abalone | LF | 105 | 17.1 | 0.8 | 301 | 85 | trace |
| Clams | LF | 80 | 11.0 | 1.5 | 80 | 40 | 0.1 |
| Mussels | LF | 75 | 12.2 | 1.6 | 80 | 25 | 0.5 |
| Octopus | LF | 76 | 15.0 | 1.5 | N/A | 122 | 0.2 |
| Oysters | LF | 70 | 14.2 | 1.2 | 75 | 50 | 0.6 |
| Scallops | LF | 82 | 15.3 | 0.2 | 160 | 50 | 0.2 |
| Squid | LF | 85 | 16.4 | 0.9 | 160 | 230 | 0.4 |
| **FISH OILS (Per Tablespoon)** | | | | | | | |
| Cod liver oil | | 129 | 0 | 14.3 | | 81 | 2.6 |
| Herring oil | | 129 | 0 | 14.3 | | 109 | 1.6 |
| Mennaden oil | | 129 | 0 | 14.3 | | 74 | 2.9 |
| MaxEPA Concentrated fish body oil | | 129 | 0 | 14.3 | | 86 | 4.2 |
| Salmon oil | | 129 | 0 | 14.3 | | 69 | 2.8 |

**NOTE:** Use these figures only as a guide. Values vary with species, water temperature, catch location, season caught, etc.

*HF — HIGH FAT FISH: over 5% fat content
 MF — MEDIUM FAT FISH: 2.5%-5% fat content
 LF — LOW FAT FISH: under 2.5% fat content
N/A — Not Available

# SHELLFISH:
# JUST WHAT THE DOCTOR ORDERED

We know that seafood is good for us. But does that include shellfish, too? The answer is absolutely yes! Shellfish are high in protein and low in total fat (1-3% fat compared to 10-30% fat in meat). Shellfish are low in calories, sodium and saturated fats, and are high in polyunsaturated fats. Omega-3 fatty acids make up a substantial portion of the fat content in shellfish, just as in fish.

There are two kinds of shellfish: mollusks and crustaceans. Mollusks are shellfish that include clams, mussels, oysters, scallops, abalone and squid. Crustaceans include lobsters, crab and shrimp. Mollusks are primarily filter feeders and eat plankton (tiny sea plants). They are vegetarians of the sea. With their diet, they contain the lowest amounts of cholesterol, ounce for ounce, of any protein source! For example, mussels have as little as 25 mg cholesterol per 3½ ounce serving. Mollusks are also rich sources of iron, copper and zinc. They are an excellent seafood choice.

One exception to low cholesterol levels in mollusks is squid. Squid contains about 230 mg cholesterol per 3½ ounce serving, in spite of its low fat content. However, in studies at the University of Washington it was found that squid does not significantly change blood triglyceride or cholesterol levels. Squid can be included in the diet in moderation.

Crustaceans are carnivorous and have a more varied diet than mollusks. Because of their diet, crustaceans have higher levels of cholesterol than mollusks. Cholesterol levels in crustaceans range from 60-160 mg cholesterol per 3½ ounce serving. Fat content is only about 1%, making crustaceans a good heart-healthy diet choice also.

Shrimp has a somewhat tarnished reputation due to a cholesterol content of about 150 mg per 3½ ounce serving. Looking at the complete nutritional picture though improves its image. Shrimp is very low in calories, total fat and saturated fat and high in polyunsaturated fats and omega-3 fatty acids. The American Heart Association allows 3½ to 4 ounces of shrimp to be eaten once per week.

The next time your doctor or dietitian recommends seafood in your diet, include shellfish, too. Your heart will love you for it!

# TASTE

Fish and seafood are naturally lean — a four-ounce portion of low fat fish or shellfish contains fewer than 100 calories — but some fish are leaner than others. The color and flavor of a fish are good indications of its fat content. Here is some general information about each type.

## □ FISH □

**LOW FAT FISH** (fat content under 2.5%)
- Generally mild flavor with tender, flaky, white or pale flesh.
- Because of a tendency to dry out during cooking, low fat fish benefit from poaching and other moist-heat cooking methods. Dry-heat methods such as baking and broiling can be used if the fish is basted with a sauce or other moist ingredients.
- Examples: cod, halibut, pollock, rockfish, grouper, flounder, sole, croaker, red snapper, lingcod, sea bass, haddock and whiting.

**MEDIUM FAT FISH** (fish content between 2.5% and 5%)
- Generally mild in flavor; pale flesh.
- Adapt well to almost all cooking methods.
- Examples: swordfish, bluefish and smelt.

**HIGH FAT FISH** (fat content over 5%)
- Generally have a firm meat-like texture, more pronounced flavor and a deeper color than low fat fish.
- Grilling, baking and other dry-heat methods are ideal for fatty fish; poaching and microwaving also give good results.
- Examples: chinook salmon, mackerel, sardines, herring, pompano and trout.

## □ SHELLFISH □

**LOW FAT SHELLFISH** (all shellfish have fat content under 2.5%)
- Generally mild in flavor.
- Adapt well to almost all cooking methods, especially microwaving.
- Examples: clams, mussels, crab and lobster.

# SEAFOOD PROFILE

Unlike most seafood charts, this profile groups together fish of similar flavor, richness and color. The different seafoods in each category taste somewhat alike and can be prepared the same way. If, for example, a recipe calls for a fish that is unavailable in your area, you can use another from the same group in its place.

## ☐ FISH ☐

### White Meat: Very light, delicate flavor
- Cod
- Dover Sole
- Haddock
- Lake Whitefish
- Orange Roughy
- Pacific Halibut
- Pacific Sanddab
- Petrale Sole
- Rex Sole
- Yellowtail Flounder
- Summer Flounder
- Yellowtail Snapper

### White Meat: Light to moderate flavor
- American Plaice/Dab
- Arrowtooth Flounder
- Butterfish
- Catfish
- English Sole
- Lingcod
- Mahi Mahi
- Pacific Whiting
- Red Snapper
- Rock Sole
- Snook
- Spotted Sea Trout
- Starry Flounder
- White King Salmon
- White Sea Trout
- Whiting
- Winter Flounder
- Wolffish

### Light Meat: Very light, delicate flavor
- Alaska Pollock
- Brook Trout
- Giant Sea Bass
- Grouper
- Pacific Ocean Perch
- Rainbow Trout
- Smelt
- Walleye
- White Sea Bass

### Light Meat: Light to moderate flavor
- Atlantic Ocean Perch
- Atlantic Salmon
- Buffalofish
- Burbot
- Carp
- Chum Salmon
- Crevalle Jack
- Croaker
- Greenland Turbot
- Jewfish
- King (Chinook) Salmon
- Lake Chub
- Lake Herring
- Lake Sturgeon
- Lake Trout
- Mako Shark
- Monkfish
- Mullet
- Northern Pike
- Perch
- Pink Salmon
- Pollock
- Pompano
- Rockfish
- Sablefish
- Sand Shark
- Scup/Porgie
- Sheepshead
- Silver (Coho) Salmon
- Striped Bass
- Swordfish

## Light Meat: More pronounced flavor
- Atlantic Mackerel
- King Mackerel
- Spanish Mackerel

## Darker Meat: Light to moderate flavor
- Black Seabass
- Sockeye (Red) Salmon
- Tuna
- Bluefish

# ☐ SHELLFISH ☐

## Crustaceans (Crab, Lobster, Shrimp)
- Alaska King Crab
- Jonah Crab
- Snow Crab
- Blue Crab
- Red Crab
- Stone Crab
- Dungeness Crab
- Soft Shell Crab

- American Lobster
- Slipper Lobster
- Spiny Lobster
- Rock Lobster

- Brown Shrimp
- Pink Shrimp
- Tiger Shrimp
- California Bay Shrimp
- Rock Shrimp
- White Shrimp
- Northern Shrimp
- Red Shrimp

## Mollusks (Clams, Scallops, Oysters, Mussels)
- Butter Clam
- Littleneck Clam
- Soft Clam/Steamer
- Geoduck Clam
- Pismo Clam
- Surf or Skinner Clam
- Hard or Quahog Clam
- Razor Clam

- Bay Scallop
- Sea Scallop
- Calico Scallop

- Eastern/Atlantic Oyster
- Olympia Oyster
- South American Oyster
- Gulf Oyster
- Pacific Oyster

- California Mussel
- Blue Mussel
- Green Shell Mussel

## Others
- Octopus
- Squid
- Crawfish
  (Freshwater Crayfish)

# SHOPPING FOR SEAFOOD

Like many other living things, fish and shellfish have their seasons. The quality of fresh seafood can depend on the size of a catch and that can depend on reproductive cycles, migratory patterns, weather conditions and water temperatures. When a particular kind of seafood is abundant the price tends to be lower than when it is scarce. Knowing when and where a particular kind of fish or shellfish is caught gives the consumer an advantage when it comes time to shop for seafood. A general knowledge of how it makes its way from the fishing boat to the seafood case is helpful.

Improved methods of handling and distribution enable delivery of fresh seafood to American consumers everywhere. Modern processing, mainly freezing, has helped reduce fluctuations in price and availability. Frozen fish and shellfish is virtually interchangeable with fresh fish and shellfish in terms of nutritive value, appearance and flavor.

# HOW TO PICK OUT THE BEST
*And Keep It That Way!*

## □ FRESH WHOLE FISH □

| GOOD QUALITY | POOR QUALITY |
|---|---|
| • Clear eyes, bright, bulging; black pupil | • Dull eyes, sunken, cloudy; gray pupil |
| • Bright red gills, free of slime; clear mucus | • Brown to grayish gills; thick, yellow mucus |
| • Flesh firm and elastic to touch, tight to bone | • Flesh soft and flabby, separating from bone |
| • Ocean-fresh odor, slight seaweed scent | • Ammonia odor, sour smell |
| • Scales adhere tightly to skin, bright color, very few missing | • Dull scales, large quantities missing |
| • Belly cavity (if gutted) clean, washed, blood-free intestinal cavity | • Belly cavity (if gutted) has cuts, bones loose from flesh, bloody, poorly cleaned |

**STORAGE:** Refrigerate, covered, at 32°F-40°F. Ice body cavity. Drain off accumulated water daily. Store 2-4 days.

## □ FRESH FILLETS/STEAKS □

| GOOD QUALITY | POOR QUALITY |
|---|---|
| • Color varies with species, but should be consistent throughout meat, bright | • Color shows bruising, red spots, yellowing or browning at edges |
| • Ocean-fresh odor, slight seaweed scent | • Ammonia odor or sour smell |
| • Clean-cut flesh, free of skin (if skinless), firm, moist | • Flesh is ragged, traces of bones and skin (if skinless), soft and mushy, dried out |
| • Packaged with tight wrapping, moist-appearing, mild odor, check date on label | • Packaged with excessive liquid, dripping, smelly, flesh folded and stuffed onto tray |

**STORAGE:** Refrigerate, covered, at 32°F-40°F. Drain off accumulated water daily. Store 2-4 days.

16

## □ CANNED SEAFOOD □

| GOOD QUALITY | POOR QUALITY |
|---|---|
| • Cans full, not dented, free from foreign matter, vacuum sealed | • Cans leaking, bulging, no vacuum seal |

**STORAGE:** Dry area. Store 6-9 months.

## □ FROZEN FISH AND SHELLFISH □

| GOOD QUALITY | POOR QUALITY |
|---|---|
| • Flesh is solidly frozen, glossy. When thawed should pass same criteria as for fresh fish or shellfish | • Flesh is partially thawed, white or dark spots, signs of drying such as papery edges, discoloration |
| • Tight, moisture-proof wrapping, complete packaging | • Packaging is punctured, shows build-up of ice crystals |
| • Should be stacked below load line of freezer case. Temperature 0° | • Improper storage; excessive glazing |

**STORAGE:** Tightly wrapped, in freezer at 0°F to -20°F. Lean fish: Store 4-6 months. Fatter fish: Store 2-3 months.

## □ LIVE SHELLFISH □

| GOOD QUALITY | POOR QUALITY |
|---|---|
| **Crabs, Lobsters, Crustaceans** | |
| • Legs move when tickled, live lobster tail curls under, heavy weight, hard shell | • No movement, lobster tail hangs limp, light weight, soft shell (except for blue soft-shelled crab) |

**STORAGE:** Keep alive in well-ventilated refrigerator in leak-proof container. Store covered with damp paper towel. Never store in airtight container as they will suffocate. Store 2-3 days.

## □ MOLLUSKS IN SHELL □

| GOOD QUALITY | POOR QUALITY |
|---|---|
| **Oysters, Mussels, Clams** | |
| • Shells tightly closed or close when tapped, clean mussels, bearded | • Gaping shells that do not close when tapped; strong, fishy odor |
| • The neck of a soft-shelled clam should twitch when touched | |

**STORAGE:** Same as crabs, lobsters, etc.

## □ SHUCKED MOLLUSKS □

| GOOD QUALITY | POOR QUALITY |
|---|---|
| • Body is plump, clear liquor, free of shell particles; liquid less than 15% of volume | • Body has a sour odor, shell particles, signs of drying, opaque liquor, excessive liquid (more than 15%) |

STORAGE: Store completely covered in leak-proof container. Oysters: Store 5-7 days. Mussels & clams: Store 2-3 days.

## □ SCALLOPS □

| GOOD QUALITY | POOR QUALITY |
|---|---|
| • Body has a creamy white to pinkish color | • Body has a sour odor; off-color |

STORAGE: Refrigerate in leak-proof, covered container with own liquid. Store 2-3 days.

## □ SHRIMP □

| GOOD QUALITY | POOR QUALITY |
|---|---|
| • Body has firm texture, mild odor, cleaned | • Body has ammonia-like odor, black spots, soft flesh |

STORAGE: Refrigerate in leak-proof container. Drain liquid. Store 3-4 days.

## □ COOKED LOBSTER, CRAB, OR SHRIMP □

| GOOD QUALITY | POOR QUALITY |
|---|---|
| • Body has mild, natural odor | • Sour odor |
| • Flesh has snowy white meat with red or brown tints (depending on species) for crab meat, bright red shell | • Flesh is slimy to the touch |
| • Kept moist, but not in direct contact with ice | |

STORAGE: Refrigerate in leak-proof container. Store 2-3 days. Pasteurized crab meat may be stored up to 6 months at 32°F, but once container is opened the crab should be used within 3-5 days.

## □ SURIMI □

| GOOD QUALITY | POOR QUALITY |
|---|---|
| • Ingredients listed | • Flesh is slimy, dull colored and has a sour odor. |

STORAGE: Refrigerate covered. Store up to one week.

# ALL SHAPES AND SIZES

Both fresh and frozen fish are marketed in quite a few different forms and it is advantageous to know them. Pick the form suggested in your recipe or the one that seems best suited to the style of preparation.

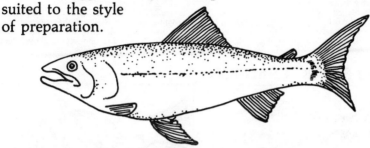

## WHOLE OR IN THE ROUND

This, as the term suggests, means the fish is whole just as it comes from the water. Nothing has been removed. The edible portion amounts to a little less than half the weight. A 1½ pound whole fish will yield about 12 edible ounces, or two to three portions.

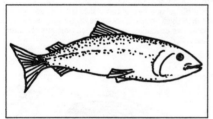

## DRAWN

The fish has been gutted. The fins and scales have usually been removed. Edible portion: 50%.

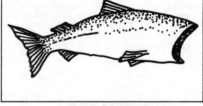

## DRESSED

The fish has been gutted and scaled, the fins removed and usually the head and tail cut off. Edible portion: 66%.

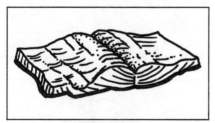

## FILLETS

Fillets are the sides of the fish cut away from the backbone. They're often boneless and skinless, though the skin of fatty fish is usually left attached to the fillets. (That way it holds together better during cooking.) Sometimes small bones called pins are present. They can be easily removed. Fillets are the most popular market form in America. Edible portion: 100%.

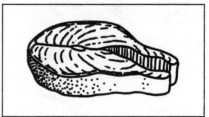

## STEAKS

These are cross-section slices, from ¾ to 1½ inches thick, of larger dressed fish. Steaks usually have a piece of the backbone in the center. Edible portion: 85%.

# HOW TO FILLET A ROUND-BODIED FISH

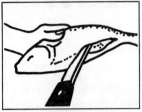
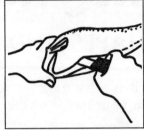
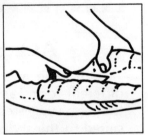

1. With fish facing away from you, use a sharp, thin-bladed knife to cut along the back of the fish, from tail to head. Make a second cut just behind the gills, down to the backbone.

2. Holding the knife at a slight angle, cut along the bone to free the back side of the fillet.

3. Peel back the free meat, then cut fillet away from rib cage. Turn fish over and repeat above steps for second fillet.

# HOW TO STEAK A SALMON

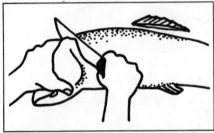
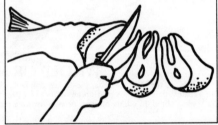

1. Remove fins from cleaned, scaled fish by running knife point along each side of fin base, then pulling fins free. To remove head, make diagonal cut behind the gills and sever backbone with heavy knife or cleaver.

2. Still using a heavy knife, slice fish into steaks about 1 inch thick, starting about 4 inches from the head end. (Reserve unsteaked head-and-tail portions for another use.)

# HOW TO FILLET A FLAT FISH

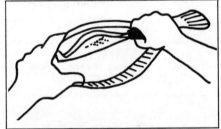

1. With the eyed (dark) side of the flatfish up, use a flexible boning knife to make a cut along the spine from the gills to the tail.

2. Slide the blade between backbone and flesh, lifting the fillet away from the bone. Remove the second fillet in the same manner.

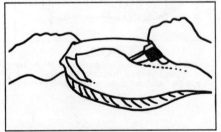
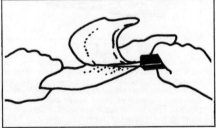

3. Turn the fish over; repeat step 2.

4. To skin, grasp fillet by the tail end, skin side down. Holding the knife at a slight angle, cut the meat free.

# HOW TO OPEN A CLAM

 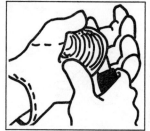 

1. Wash clams thoroughly, discarding any that have broken shells or that do not close. Wearing a heavy glove for safety, hold the clam in your palm and force the blade of a clam knife between the shells.

2. Run the knife around the edge of the shell to cut through the muscles holding it together.

3. Open clam and remove top shell. Use knife to loosen clam from bottom shell. Check for shell fragments before serving.

# HOW TO SHUCK AN OYSTER

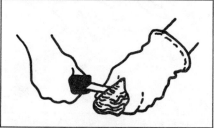 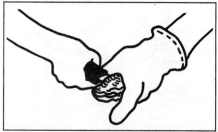

1. Hold oysters under cold running water and scrub with a stiff brush; discard those that are not tightly closed or that do not close quickly when handled. Place oyster, cupped side down, on a firm surface, holding it (with a gloved hand) near the hinge.

2. Insert an oyster knife in the side opposite the hinge, and twist knife blade to force oyster open.

3. Run the knife around the edge of the shell to cut the muscle that holds the two shells together.

4. Remove top shell, and loosen oyster from bottom shell. Check for shell fragments before serving.

# HOW TO CLEAN A MUSSEL

1. Prepare mussels as soon as possible after gathering. If mussels must be stored, refrigerate them at 35°F to 40°F. To prepare, scrub shells in cold water to remove grass and mud. Discard those that have open shells or shells that do not close quickly with handling.

2. Clip or pull beard; rinse mussel before cooking.

21

# HOW TO DRESS A SOFT-SHELL CRAB

 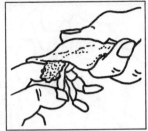 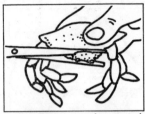

1. Remove the apron, the segmented abdominal part beneath the carapace, or shell.

2. Lift the carapace's pointed ends, and remove spongy material.

3. Using scissors, cut about ½ inch behind the eyes and remove the face of the crab. What remains is the edible portion.

# HOW TO CRACK A CRAB

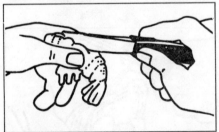 

1. To remove back, hold the crab in one hand, pry off the shell with the other.

2. Using a small, heavy knife, cut away the gills. Wash out the intestines and spongy matter.

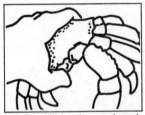 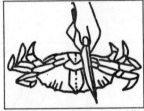 

3. Break off the claws and crack them with the knife handle, a mallet, or the back of a cleaver. Use the knife to pry meat out if necessary. Twist legs loose from the body, crack them, and remove meat.

4. Cut the body down the middle, then cut halves into several parts. Use the point of the knife to remove the lump of meat from each side of the rear portion of the body.

5. Remove the remainder of the meat by prying upward with the knife.

# HOW TO CLEAN A SHRIMP

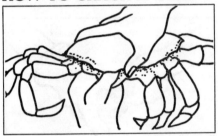 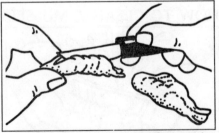

1. With a sharp knife, make a shallow cut along the back of the shrimp, from head to tail. Peel off shell and legs, leaving the shell on the tail, if desired. To devein, hold shrimp under cold running water. The water will help rinse out the vein.

2. To butterfly, cut along the back of the shrimp, but not all the way through. Spread the halves open.

# HOW TO DRESS A LOBSTER

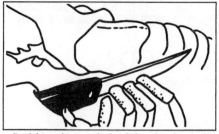

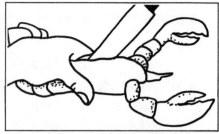

1. For lobster that is to be broiled, rather than boiled live. Cut off legs.

2. Insert a knife in the abdomen, and cut through the undershell toward the head, leaving back shell intact.

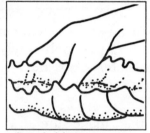

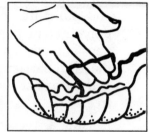

3. Cut toward the tail.

4. Press the lobster apart.

5. Remove sand sac from head; remove intestinal tract.

# HOW TO DRESS A SQUID

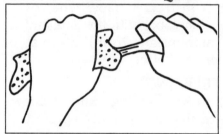

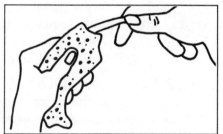

1. Pull tentacles firmly but slowly from outer body sac, leaving body intact. Intestines should come out with tentacles.

2. From body sac, pull out and discard thin, transparent quill.

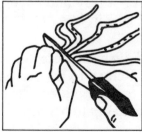

3. Peel away speckled outer membrane covering sac and fins. Turn body sac inside out, and rinse.

4. Cut tentacles off where they join head, and discard head.

5. The tube may be stuffed or sliced, the tentacles chopped and included in stuffing or in a marinated salad.

# FROZEN SEAFOOD

- **WRAPPING SEAFOOD FOR FREEZING**
Two recommended ways to freeze seafood
are wrapping and glazing. Not all materials
are good for wrapping and freezing seafood.
Aluminum foil, for example, does not seal well
and punctures easily. Wax paper, cellophane and
polyethylene plastic bags are also not suitable. Plastic
bags and wrap made of pvc (polyvinyl chloride) provide
the ideal barrier to water vapor and air. Check the labeling
and purchase wraps and bags specifically designed for
freezing.

If using a freezer bag, make sure all the air is pressed out
before sealing. If using a wrap, wrap very tightly to eliminate
any air pockets; the wrap should form a tight skin.
Wrap the package with freezer paper, foil, or
place in plastic bag; then label with the date and
contents (type of fish, amount and form). Store at
0°F to -20°F. The colder the better.

- **GLAZING SEAFOOD FOR FREEZING**
Wrapping is the easiest method for freezing seafood but
glazing with water makes an effective shield of ice to protect
the seafood from oxidation and dehydration.

- **TO GLAZE WITH WATER FOLLOW THESE STEPS:**
Lay pieces of fish on a tray and cover with aluminum foil
or waxed paper. Place in freezer. As soon as fish is hard,
remove.

Remove cover and dip each piece quickly in ice-cold water;
a glaze will form. Return to freezer, uncovered, to let the
film harden for 5 to 10 minutes. Repeat the process until
a thick glaze is formed (up to 6 times). Wrap, label and place
package in freezer.

- **THAWING FROZEN SEAFOOD**
  If the fish is to be defrosted, run it under cold water with its wrapping intact. Never defrost under warm water or at room temperature because spoilage may occur. Another safe method to defrost is to refrigerate frozen seafood allowing approximately one day per pound of seafood.
- **THAWING FROZEN SEAFOOD IN THE MICROWAVE**
  Frozen seafood also may be thawed in a microwave oven. Follow the manufacturer's recommendations for defrosting. The size and weight of the portion affects thawing time. Whole fish, packaged seafood and larger cuts of fish should be turned over midway through the cycle. Shellfish should be thawed quickly and carefully to prevent overheating.

For best results, use the on-off method to defrost fish and shellfish in the microwave:

**1.** Microwave seafood for 15 to 30 seconds on medium-low (30% power or the defrost setting). Let the seafood rest for 15 seconds. Rotate dish.

**2.** Continue to alternate microwaving and resting until the seafood is nearly thawed but still quite cold to the touch.

**3.** Allow seafood to rest for 1 to 2 minutes before cooking.

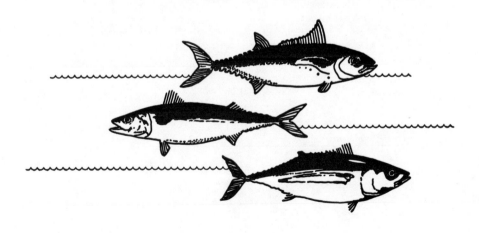

# APPETIZERS

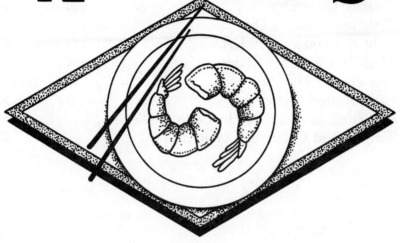

CHAPTER 2

## CHAPTER 2
# APPETIZERS

# SALMON CHEESECAKE
*Wonderful for Sunday brunch or buffet item*

- ☐ 20 low salt Ritz or Saltine crackers, crumbled
- ☐ 2 packages (8 oz. each) light cream cheese
- ☐ 1 cup part-skim Ricotta cheese
- ☐ 2 eggs
- ☐ ¼ cup canned evaporated skim milk
- ☐ 1 T. onion, minced
- ☐ ⅛ tsp. white pepper
- ☐ ½ tsp. liquid smoke
- ☐ 1 can (15½ oz.) pink salmon, drained
- ☐ Parsley, chopped

1. Sprinkle Ritz cracker crumbs evenly over bottom of springform pan or in ring mold.
2. Beat light cream cheese, Ricotta cheese, eggs, canned evaporated skim milk and onions in large bowl at medium speed, scraping bowl occasionally, until smooth, about 5 minutes.
3. Fold in white pepper, liquid smoke and drained canned salmon.
4. Spoon into pan. Bake for 45 minutes at 375⁰. Garnish with parsley, serve with fresh fruit plate and green salad. **Makes 12-16 servings.**

*145 calories per serving*
*8.0 grams fat per serving*
*310 mg sodium per serving*
*101 mg cholesterol per serving*

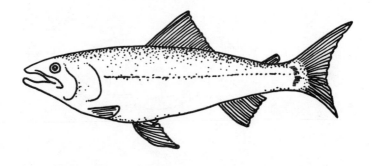

# LOMI LOMI-SALMON HAWAIIAN STYLE
*A Hawaiian favorite*

- ☐ 1 can (15½ oz.) salmon
- ☐ 3 tomatoes, diced
- ☐ ⅔ cup green onion, thinly sliced
- ☐ 2 T. salmon liquid
- ☐ 2 tsp. lemon juice

1. Drain salmon, reserving liquid. Flake salmon.
2. Combine salmon, tomatoes, onion, salmon liquid and lemon juice; mix well. Chill overnight. Can be served before or with dinner. **Makes 12 servings.**

*70 calories per serving*
*3.3 grams fat per serving*
*200 mg sodium per serving*
*20 mg cholesterol per serving*

# CREAMY CLAM DIP

☐ 4 oz. light cream cheese
☐ 1 pint low fat cottage cheese
☐ 3 T. lemon juice
☐ 2 tsp. horseradish
☐ ¼ tsp. hot pepper sauce (Tabasco)

☐ ¼ cup green onion, chopped
☐ 1 can (6½ oz.) clams, minced and drained

1. In mixer, food processor or blender beat light cream cheese and cottage cheese together until smooth.
2. Add lemon juice, horseradish and Tabasco. Mix to blend flavors.
3. Remove dip from mixer and mix in green onion and drained clams by hand. Serve in hollowed-out red cabbage head. Serve with assorted fresh vegetables. **Makes 2 cups.**

*28 calories per tablespoon*
*1.0 gram fat per tablespoon*
*69 mg sodium per tablespoon*
*6 mg cholesterol per tablespoon*

**Substitutions:**
crab meat, shrimp meat

# FLINTSTONE SEAFOOD DIP

*Great to munch on during sporting events.*
*Take to a tailgate party.*

- ☐ 1 pint low fat cottage cheese, blended
- ☐ 1 cup Dill Dressing (see page 33 )
- ☐ 1 pkg. (10 oz.) frozen spinach, chopped, thawed and thoroughly drained
- ☐ 1 can (8 oz.) water chestnuts, drained and chopped
- ☐ ½ lb. imitation crab
- ☐ Flintstone bread

1. Blend cottage cheese until smooth. Mix with Dill Dressing in bowl.
2. Squeeze thawed spinach to remove all water and add to cottage cheese mixture. Add water chestnuts and shrimp or crab and mix thoroughly.
3. If thinner consistency is desired, add more Dill Dressing. Refrigerate to let flavors blend.
4. Cut top off Flintstone bread or any other round loaf of bread. Hollow out and fill with dip. Serve with bread cubes (from middle of hollowed bread). Dip may also be eaten with raw cut vegetables or crackers. **Makes 4 cups of dip.**

*15 calories per tablespoon*
*0.5 gram fat per tablespoon*
*42 mg sodium per tablespoon*
*3 mg cholesterol per tablespoon*

**Substitutions:**
crab meat, shrimp meat

# LIGHT & VERSATILE DILL DRESSING

- ☐ 2 cups plain low fat yogurt
- ☐ 3 T. mayonnaise
- ☐ 1 T. skim milk
- ☐ 1 T. green onion, chopped
- ☐ ¼ tsp. dried dill weed
- ☐ ⅛ tsp. celery salt
- ☐ ⅛ tsp. onion powder
- ☐ ½ tsp. parsley flakes

1. Mix yogurt, mayonnaise and milk until blended. Stir in remaining ingredients. Refrigerate. Make ahead and use as a salad dressing, topping on baked potatoes, or in Flintstone Seafood Dip (see page 32 ). **Makes 2 cups dressing.**

*18 calories per tablespoon*
*2.5 grams fat per tablespoon*
*36 mg sodium per tablespoon*
*1 mg cholesterol per tablespoon*

# ALECK BAY STEAMER CLAMS

*Aleck Bay steamers are dug only on Lopez Island in the San Juan Islands of Washington State. Other clams work well, too!*

- [ ] **20 steamer clams in shell**
- [ ] **1 cup water**
- [ ] **1 cup white wine**
- [ ] **1 T. polyunsaturated margarine**
- [ ] **2 cups dry bread crumbs**
- [ ] **1½ tsp. Worcestershire sauce**
- [ ] **2 cloves garlic, minced**
- [ ] **1 tsp. dry mustard**
- [ ] **¼ tsp. hot pepper sauce (Tabasco)**
- [ ] **¼ cup parsley, chopped**
- [ ] **Paprika**

1. Scrub the clams and rinse under cold water. Place clams in kettle and cover clams with water and wine. Steam clams just until they open. Remove from kettle. Save nectar. Discard any clams that do not open.
2. When clams are cooled, remove from shell and chop medium fine.
3. In skillet, melt margarine and lightly toss the clams with bread crumbs, Worcestershire sauce, garlic, mustard, Tabasco and parsley. Let bread crumbs absorb the margarine mixture; add a little nectar to keep the mixture slightly moist.
4. Stuff shells; top lightly with paprika. Bake 5 minutes in 400° oven, or until warmed through. Serve with nectar. **Makes 4 servings.**

*291 calories per serving*
*4.0 grams fat per serving*
*248 mg sodium per serving*
*16 mg cholesterol per serving*

**Substitutions:**
clams, mussels in shell

# MUSSELS ON THE HALF-SHELL

 *To keep seafood in the shell from tipping over while cooking, place shells on a bed of crumpled foil on a flat cookie sheet.*

- ☐ 6 lbs. mussels in shell
- ☐ 1 cup water
- ☐ 1 cup dry, white wine
- ☐ 2½ T. olive oil
- ☐ ½ cup onion, minced
- ☐ ½ cup red bell pepper, finely minced
- ☐ ½ cup celery, finely minced
- ☐ ¼ cup green onion, finely minced
- ☐ 2 T. Dijon mustard
- ☐ Cayenne pepper to taste
- ☐ ½ cup Italian-style bread crumbs

1. Scrub mussels and pull out beards. Steam in large covered pot in boiling water and wine, just until shells open. Remove from heat and cool.
2. Remove mussels from their shells. Save half the shells.
3. In a medium skillet over medium heat, heat the olive oil and add onion, red pepper, celery and green onion and saute until softened. Stir in mustard. Add mussel meat and cayenne pepper. Remove from heat.
4. Fill each shell with a mussel and a little of the vegetable mixture. Sprinkle with bread crumbs and bake in 400° oven until browned (about 5 minutes). **Makes 12 servings.**

*123 calories per appetizer*
*4.6 grams fat per appetizer*
*136 mg sodium per appetizer*
*22 mg cholesterol per appetizer*

**Substitutions:**
clams in shell, oysters in shell

# HERB STUFFED OYSTERS

☐ 12 large oysters in shell

☐ 1 pkg. (10 oz.) frozen spinach, chopped and thawed

☐ 1 T. polyunsaturated margarine

☐ 2 T. onion, finely minced

☐ ¼ cup fresh parsley, chopped

☐ 1 T. dried tarragon

☐ 2 T. lemon juice

☐ Hot pepper sauce to taste (Tabasco)

☐ Pepper to taste

☐ 2 T. Parmesan cheese

1. Place bottom shell of oysters in a single layer in a 9" x 13" baking dish. Place one oyster on each shell.
2. Squeeze all of the moisture out of spinach.
3. Melt margarine in a medium-size skillet over medium-high heat. Add onion and saute until soft, about 5 minutes.
4. Add spinach, parsley, and tarragon and cook 2-3 minutes; stirring frequently.
5. Top each oyster with a generous tablespoon of the spinach mixture, and sprinkle each with a little Parmesan cheese. Season with Tabasco and pepper.
6. Bake at 450⁰ until cheese is golden brown, about 10 minutes. **Makes 12 appetizers.**

*48 calories per appetizer*
*1.6 grams fat per appetizer*
*68 mg sodium per appetizer*
*20 mg cholesterol per appetizer*

**Substitutions:**
mussels, clams

# BAY SCALLOPS & SHRIMP IN PASTA SHELLS

♥ *In many of our recipes we use blended cottage cheese. To blend cottage cheese, use food processor or blender and process until creamy.*

## SALAD:

☐ 1 cup bay scallops, steamed, cooled and drained

☐ 1 cup shrimp, cooked, peeled and deveined

☐ 1 cup celery, finely chopped

☐ ¼ cup green onion, chopped

☐ ¼ cup low fat cottage cheese, blended

☐ 1 T. lemon juice

☐ 1 T. fresh dill, chopped

☐ White pepper to taste

## PASTA:
6 oz. large pasta shells
1 T. low calorie Italian dressing

1. To make salad: toss salad ingredients together. Adjust seasoning to taste.
2. To make pasta: bring 1 quart of water to boil. Carefully add pasta and boil uncovered about 10-12 minutes, stirring occasionally. Cool shells under running water. Drain and blend gently with low calorie dressing.
3. Spoon scallop and shrimp salad into shells. **Makes 5 servings.**

*200 calories per serving*
*1.5 grams fat per serving*
*160 mg sodium per serving*
*77 mg cholesterol per serving*

**Substitutions:**
lobster meat, crab meat, imitation crab

# SHRIMP AND CUCUMBER SALAD

- ☐ 1 T. light soy sauce
- ☐ 1 T. polyunsaturated oil
- ☐ ⅛ tsp. dried ginger or ½ tsp. fresh ginger, sliced
- ☐ 1 cup shrimp, cooked, peeled and deveined, chopped
- ☐ 2 green onions, finely chopped
- ☐ 1 medium rib celery, finely chopped
- ☐ 2 medium cucumbers, peeled and thinly sliced

1. In small bowl mix soy sauce, oil and ginger. Add shrimp and green onions. Toss until well coated. Marinate in refrigerator for 20 minutes.
2. Slice celery and cucumbers and place on serving tray. Arrange shrimp mixture over top of vegetables. Pour marinade over all. Excellent as a buffet salad served with steamed rice and sushi with pickled ginger. **Makes 4 servings.**

*78 calories per serving*
*3.9 grams fat per serving*
*252 mg sodium per serving*
*50 mg cholesterol per serving*

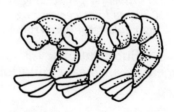

# SALADS

## CHAPTER 3
# SALADS

# MARINATED HALIBUT SALAD

- ☐ ¼ cup white wine vinegar
- ☐ 4 tsp. sugar
- ☐ 1 T. olive oil
- ☐ ¼ tsp. dried dill weed
- ☐ ½ bay leaf
- ☐ 5 peppercorns
- ☐ 1 lb. halibut, boneless, skinless, cut into 1-inch chunks
- ☐ ½ onion, thinly sliced
- ☐ ½ lemon, thinly sliced
- ☐ Lettuce
- ☐ 12 cherry tomatoes
- ☐ 1 small cucumber, sliced

## MICROWAVE:

1. In 1-quart microwave-proof bowl combine vinegar, sugar, oil and seasonings; mix well. Microwave, covered, on HIGH for 1-2 minutes or until mixture boils.
2. Add halibut. Microwave, covered, on HIGH for 2-3 minutes, or until fish just barely flakes; gently stir halfway through cooking time.
3. Layer fish, onion and lemon in small bowl; pour cooking liquid over all. Refrigerate, covered, overnight.
4. Drain and serve on lettuce-lined salad platter with tomatoes and cucumber slices. **Makes 4 servings.**

*217 calories per serving*
*5.0 grams fat per serving*
*73 mg sodium per serving*
*56 mg cholesterol per serving*

**Substitutions:**
swordfish, shark, monkfish

# TARRAGON SALMON SALAD

 *When cooked and flaked fish is needed for a recipe, you can use leftovers or microwave or steam fresh or frozen fillets.*

**Directions for microwaving are as follows:**
*Place fillets on a microwave-proof roasting rack and brush with lemon juice and olive oil. Cover with waxed paper or microwave plastic wrap. Microwave on HIGH for 2-4 minutes or until fish flakes.*

- ☐ 1 can (7 oz.) salmon, drained
- ☐ ⅓ cup celery, chopped
- ☐ ¼ cup green onion, minced
- ☐ ¼ cup radishes, chopped
- ☐ 3 T. Tarragon-Mustard Sauce (see page 129)
- ☐ 2 T. fresh parsley, minced
- ☐ 1 tsp. lemon juice
- ☐ Lettuce leaves

1. Break salmon into bite-size pieces.
2. Combine salmon with celery, onion and radishes in bowl; set aside.
3. Combine Tarragon-Mustard Sauce, parsley, and lemon juice in bowl and stir well. Add to salmon mixture; toss gently to coat. Cover and chill.
4. Serve on lettuce-lined plates. **Makes 4 servings.**

*122 calories per serving*
*5.5 grams fat per serving*
*288 mg sodium per serving*
*31 mg cholesterol per serving*

**Substitutions:**
any cooked and flaked seafood, water-packed tuna

# SWEET AND SOUR TUNA SALAD

*The most popular seafood species consumed in the U.S. to date were tuna, shrimp and codfish, in that order. These three constituted more than half the total seafood consumption.*

- ☐ 1 can (6½ oz.) water-packed tuna
- ☐ ¼ cup red wine vinegar
- ☐ 1 T. sugar
- ☐ 1 T. lemon juice
- ☐ 1 tsp. lemon peel, grated
- ☐ Dash cayenne pepper

- ☐ 1 T. olive oil
- ☐ 1 medium zucchini, thinly sliced and quartered
- ☐ ½ cup green onion, diagonally sliced
- ☐ 2 T. fresh parsley, chopped
- ☐ Tomato wedges

1. Drain and flake tuna in bowl.
2. Heat vinegar and sugar in saucepan until sugar is dissolved. Remove from heat and cool slightly.
3. Add lemon juice and peel, cayenne pepper and olive oil.
4. Combine zucchini, green onion, parsley, tuna and vinegar mixture. Marinate 1 hour or longer. Drain before serving, if desired. Serve with tomato wedges. **Makes 4 servings.**

*133 calories per serving*
*5.0 grams fat per serving*
*179 mg sodium per serving*
*15 mg cholesterol per serving*

**Substitutions:**
canned salmon, shrimp, imitation crab

# GREEK-STYLE SALAD

 *To reduce the amount of sodium in canned salmon or tuna by half, rinse in colander under cold water.*

## DRESSING:

- ☐ 1 T. olive oil
- ☐ 3 T. lemon juice
- ☐ 1 tsp. dried dill weed
- ☐ ⅛ tsp. red pepper, crushed
- ☐ ½ tsp. pepper
- ☐ ¼ tsp. garlic powder
- ☐ 2 ozs. Feta cheese, grated
- ☐ 1 can (6½ oz.) water-packed tuna, undrained

## SALAD GREENS:

*Here are a few suggestions.*
*Any combination of vegetables are great!*

- ☐ ½ head shredded cabbage or shredded lettuce
- ☐ 1 tomato, thinly sliced
- ☐ 1 cucumber, thinly sliced
- ☐ ½ red, yellow or green pepper, chopped
- ☐ 1 carrot, grated

1. To prepare dressing: whisk ingredients together in medium-size bowl.
2. Place in refrigerator to blend flavors while preparing salad greens.
3. To prepare salad greens: layer vegetables. Spoon dressing over bed of vegetables. Garnish. **Makes 4 servings.**

*171 calories per serving*
*7.5 grams fat per serving*
*39 mg sodium per serving*
*28.5 mg cholesterol per serving*

**Substitutions:**
canned sardines, cooked halibut,
imitation crab, canned salmon

# SEA SHELL SALAD

 *The only pasta that contains cholesterol is egg noodles. A serving (1 cup cooked, 2 ounces dry) has about 70 mg cholesterol, about one-quarter of the daily recommended maximum, so avoid using egg noodles.*

- ☐ 3 stalks broccoli or 1 pkg. (10 oz.) frozen broccoli, thawed
- ☐ 8 ozs. dry macaroni shells
- ☐ ½ red onion, finely chopped
- ☐ 2 cloves garlic, minced
- ☐ 2 T. lemon juice or juice of 1 lemon
- ☐ 2 tsp. Italian Seafood Seasoning (see page 138)
- ☐ 1 T. olive oil
- ☐ ¼ cup Parmesan cheese
- ☐ ¼ tsp. pepper
- ☐ 2 cans (6½ oz. each) water-packed tuna, drained

1. Peel broccoli stems; slice. Steam broccoli until tender-crisp.
2. Cook macaroni shells as per instructions on package until just tender; drain.
3. In medium-size bowl, mix together onion, garlic, lemon juice, Italian Seafood Seasoning, olive oil, Parmesan cheese and black pepper.
4. Toss with warm shells and broccoli. Chill.
5. Add tuna before serving and toss. **Makes 6-8 servings.**

*207 calories per serving*
*4.2 grams fat per serving*
*244 mg sodium per serving*
*26 mg cholesterol per serving*

**Substitutions:**
canned salmon

# CHINESE SEAFOOD SALAD

*Great for a potluck*

 *Be sure to read label of chow mein noodles. Choose a brand made without hydrogenated oil or shortening.*

### DRESSING:

☐ 3 T. light soy sauce

☐ 1 T. polyunsaturated vegetable oil

☐ 2 T. rice vinegar

☐ ½ tsp. sesame oil

☐ ½ tsp. garlic powder

☐ ½ tsp. pepper

### SALAD:

☐ 3 cups lettuce, shredded

☐ 1 can (6½ oz.) water-packed tuna, drained

☐ ¼ cup red cabbage, chopped

☐ ½ cup carrots, julienne cut

☐ ¼ cup green onion, diagonally sliced

☐ 1 can (8 oz.) sliced water chestnuts, drained

☐ ½ cup chow mein noodles, uncooked, crumbled

1. To make dressing: in large bowl, whisk ingredients together.
2. Add lettuce, tuna and vegetables. Toss with dressing.
3. Top with chow mein noodles and serve. **Makes 6 servings.**

*155 calories per serving*
*4.6 grams fat per serving*
*536 mg sodium per serving*
*20 mg cholesterol per serving*

**Substitutions:**
any cooked, flaked seafood

# PASTA & CRAB SALAD

- ☐ 8 ozs. dry pasta, such as sea shells
- ☐ 1¼ cups low fat cottage cheese, blended
- ☐ 2 tsp. dried basil
- ☐ ¾ tsp. pepper
- ☐ 1 clove garlic, minced

- ☐ ½ cup green pepper, chopped
- ☐ ⅓ cup red onion, finely chopped
- ☐ ½ cucumber, peeled, sliced and quartered
- ☐ 1 lb. imitation crab, flaked

1. Prepare noodles according to package directions. Drain.
2. Blend cottage cheese. Add basil, pepper and garlic.
3. Prepare vegetables. Chop green pepper, red onion, and slice cucumber.
4. Toss all ingredients together in large bowl with imitation crab.
5. Serve warm or chilled. **Makes 8 cups or 16 servings.**

*105 calories per half cup*
*1.0 gram fat per half cup*
*210 mg sodium per half cup*
*21 mg cholesterol per half cup*

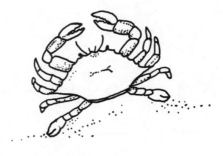

# SENSATIONAL SEAFOOD SALAD

- ☐ ¾ cup low fat cottage cheese, blended
- ☐ ½ cup part-skim Mozzarella cheese, grated
- ☐ ⅓ cup green onion, finely chopped
- ☐ ½ cup frozen peas
- ☐ ½ cup green cabbage, grated

- ☐ ¼ cup black olives, chopped
- ☐ ½ cup carrots, grated
- ☐ 6 drops hot pepper sauce (Tabasco)
- ☐ 2 tsp. Worcestershire sauce
- ☐ 12 oz. imitation crab, shredded
- ☐ Lettuce leaves

1. Place all ingredients in bowl and toss together.
2. Serve on a bed of lettuce. **Makes 4 cups or 8 servings.**

*110 calories per serving*
*3.3 grams fat per serving*
*383 mg sodium per serving*
*30 mg cholesterol per serving*

**Substitutions:**
any cooked, flaked seafood

# CILANTRO POTATO SALAD

*Great make-ahead idea for a party or barbecue*

- ☐ 3 lbs. new potatoes, scrubbed (about 12 med.)
- ☐ ¾ cup plain low fat yogurt
- ☐ ½ cup shallots or green onions, chopped
- ☐ 1 cup celery, chopped

- ☐ ¼ cup fresh cilantro, finely chopped
- ☐ 2 T. Dijon mustard
- ☐ 2 T. red wine vinegar
- ☐ ½ tsp. pepper
- ☐ 12 oz. imitation crab or other leftover seafood

1. Cook potatoes in boiling water or steam on rack over boiling water until tender. Let cool to room temperature. Peel and cut into chunks.
2. Combine remaining ingredients in large bowl. Add potatoes and stir to mix well. Taste and adjust seasonings.
3. Serve at room temperature or refrigerate and serve slightly chilled. **Makes 8 servings.**

*190 calories per serving*
*0.5 gram fat per serving*
*317 mg sodium per serving*
*21 mg cholesterol per serving*

# MARINATED SPANISH SEAFOOD SALAD

☐ 2 large tomatoes, seeded
☐ 1 lb. bay scallops
☐ ½ lb. medium prawns, peeled and deveined
☐ 1 medium red bell pepper, seeded and diced
☐ ½ tsp. dried red pepper flakes
☐ 1 T. red onion, minced
☐ 8 T. fresh lime juice

☐ 2 T. olive oil
☐ 1 clove garlic, minced
☐ ½ tsp. sweet Hungarian paprika
☐ ½ tsp. salt
☐ Pepper to taste
☐ 2 T. fresh cilantro, finely chopped
☐ 6 large lettuce leaves
☐ 1 lime, cut into 6 wedges

1. Cut tomatoes into large cubes; set aside.
2. Bring pan of water to boiling, add scallops and simmer gently for 3 minutes. Remove with slotted spoon and rinse with cold water to stop cooking. Bring water back to boil, add prawns and simmer for 3-4 minutes, or until pink and curled. Drain and rinse with cold water.
3. Place seafood in bowl and add tomatoes, red bell pepper, red pepper flakes and onion. Whisk together lime juice, olive oil, garlic, paprika, salt and pepper. Reserve 2 T. of dressing and pour remaining dressing over salad. Stir the cilantro into the salad and refrigerate for at least 1 hour. Stir occasionally.
4. Arrange lettuce leaves on 6 large plates. Transfer salad to the plates with slotted spoon. Drizzle 1 tsp. of dressing over each salad and garnish with wedge of lime. **Makes 8-10 servings.**

*106 calories per serving*
*3.4 grams fat per serving*
*140 mg sodium per serving*
*36 mg cholesterol per serving*

# CURRY SHRIMP AND RICE SALAD

- ☐ 3 cups steamed rice
- ☐ 2 cans (6½ oz. each) shrimp or ¾ lb. shrimp, cooked, peeled and deveined
- ☐ 1 cup celery, chopped
- ☐ 2 green onions, chopped
- ☐ 1 apple, diced
- ☐ ¼ cup slivered almonds, chopped
- ☐ 1½ tsp. curry
- ☐ 1 tsp. paprika
- ☐ Pepper to taste
- ☐ ¼ cup raisins
- ☐ Vanilla low fat yogurt to moisten

1. Mix ingredients together and serve. **Makes 6-8 servings.**

*178 calories per serving*
*3.5 grams fat per serving*
*91 mg sodium per serving*
*50 mg cholesterol per serving*

**Substitutions:**
canned water-packed tuna, canned salmon, crab meat

# SHRIMP COLESLAW

## SALAD:

- ☐ 1 medium head cabbage, cored and shredded
- ☐ 1 small green pepper, seeded and diced
- ☐ 1 medium carrot, peeled and minced
- ☐ 2 medium green onions, finely chopped
- ☐ 2 cups small cooked shrimp

## DRESSING:

- ☐ 1 cup plain low fat yogurt
- ☐ ¼ cup fresh dill, finely chopped
- ☐ 3 T. cider vinegar
- ☐ 1 tsp. sugar
- ☐ ½ tsp. pepper
- ☐ ½ tsp. celery seed
- ☐ ½ tsp. Dijon mustard

1. To prepare salad: in large bowl combine cabbage, green pepper, carrot, green onions and shrimp.
2. To make dressing: stir together yogurt, dill, vinegar, sugar, pepper, celery seed and mustard.
3. Mix with salad and chill for 1 hour or until ready to serve. **Makes 10 servings.**

*30 calories per serving*
*0.6 gram fat per serving*
*63 mg sodium per serving*
*40 mg cholesterol per serving*

**Substitutions:**
imitation crab

# SOUPS &

# SANDWICHES

CHAPTER 4

## CHAPTER 4
# SOUPS AND SANDWICHES

# SEAFOOD IS KID FOOD

Every child loves the feel of a wiggly fish on the end of his fishin' pole, but to convince him to eat it is often another story! With a little ingenuity you can help your family (kids, too!) become avid seafood fans.

- **START CHILDREN EARLY!**
Seafood is an ideal first protein source for toddlers. It is easy to chew and digest. Seafood is perfect as a finger food. With its mild flavor it is often more easily accepted by youngsters than red meat.

- **ONE-POT MEALS ARE GOOD!**
A quick and easy one-pot meal to start a toddler is seafood poached in a liquid such as chicken broth or seasoned water. Start with diced potatoes and a favorite vegetable. Cover with liquid and simmer until tender. Add fish chunks and steam until fish flakes when tested with a fork.

- **CHOOSE BONELESS FISH.**
Sometimes toddlers and younger children are afraid of bones. So choose boneless and skinless fillets or ask your seafood retailer to debone fish. Good boneless finger foods are shrimp, imitation crab, and squid.

- **START SLOWLY.**
Serve one seafood meal per week to your family and increase gradually. For the first few meals, serve a meal of their favorite dishes and a small portion of seafood.

*"Seafood is fingerfood"*

- **GET THE KIDS INVOLVED.**
  Get the children involved in preparation of seafood meals. They are often enthusiastic helpers. Peeling shrimp, picking crab or debearding mussels are all fun chores. Encourage the kids to be part of the shopping trip. All kids love to look at the live crab and lobster tank in many seafood departments. Let them decide what type of seafood they might like to try for dinner.

  Have the kids help with the actual cooking, too. Chopping vegetables or cutting fish into chunks, with supervision, can help win them over. Let the kids help make their favorite dessert for the end of the seafood dinner. Serve recipes with familiar flavors. Try "Italian Fisherman's Spaghetti", always a favorite with its tomato base and Italian flavors.

- **IT'S A LIFETIME DIET.**
  Let seafood join your family's meal plan at least three times per week. It is important to get children off to an early start with a heart-healthy diet that may help prevent heart disease later in life. Children may surprise their parents and actually look forward to "Manhattan Shellfish Chowder" or poached salmon! Seafood is the perfect kid food!

  Suggested recipes: Lunchbox Tuna Sandwich, page 57
  Italian Fisherman's Spaghetti, page 96
  Four-Minute Flounder, page 110

♥ *Seafood eating is fun with a hint from a fisherman's wife: keep a jar of pennies by the table for your seafood dinners. Have the kids "go fishin' " for the bones. With every bone, a penny is earned. Kids will gladly clean their plates.*

*"Go fishin' for bones"*

# LUNCHBOX TUNA OR SALMON SANDWICH

*It's fun to have a variety of breads on hand in the freezer. This sandwich spread is great in pita bread, on rye, whole grain breads or spread on rice cakes.*

- □ 1 can (6½ oz.) water-packed tuna or salmon
- □ ½ cup low fat cottage cheese, blended
- □ 3 T. celery, finely chopped
- □ 2 T. green onion, finely chopped
- □ 8 slices of bread

- □ Suggested garnishes:
  sliced tomatoes
  sliced cucumbers
  sliced pickle
  alfalfa sprouts
  lettuce

1. Drain and flake tuna or salmon with a fork.
2. Combine fish, cottage cheese and vegetables.
3. Use ¼ of mixture for each of 4 sandwiches. Garnish as desired. Serve with fresh fruit. **Makes 4 sandwiches.**

*WITH TUNA:*
*217 calories per sandwich*
*6.0 grams fat per sandwich*
*484 mg sodium per sandwich*
*24 mg cholesterol per sandwich*

*WITH SALMON:*
*240 calories per sandwich*
*3.0 grams fat per sandwich*
*580 mg sodium per sandwich*
*48 mg cholesterol per sandwich*

**Substitutions:**
any cooked, flaked fish

# TUNA MELT SUPREME

♥ *Solid white albacore tuna is one of the best sources of omega-3 fatty acids. The canning process does not significantly reduce the omega-3 content in canned tuna or other varieties of canned seafood such as canned salmon. Chunk light tuna has only half of the amount of omega-3's as in the solid white variety. Tuna packed in water has the same omega-3 content as tuna packed in oil. But, while draining water from water-packed tuna removes only about 3% of the omega-3's, draining oil removes 15-25% (because these fatty acids are oil-soluble).*

☐ 1 can (6½ oz.) water-packed tuna, drained
☐ ¼ cup low fat cottage cheese, blended
☐ ¼ cup carrot, grated
☐ 1 T. red onion, minced
☐ 1 tsp. lemon juice

☐ ½ tsp. capers, drained
☐ ¼ tsp. Dijon mustard
☐ ⅛ tsp. pepper
☐ 2 English muffins, split and toasted
☐ 2 oz. part-skim Mozzarella cheese, grated

**MICROWAVE:**

1. Combine all ingredients except muffin and cheese.
2. Spoon tuna mixture onto muffin halves and top with cheese.
3. Place on paper towel on microwave-proof plate. Microwave on HIGH until cheese is melted, about 35-45 seconds. Garnish with a little grated carrot and serve hot. **Makes 4 open-faced sandwiches.**

*184 calories per sandwich*
*4.1 grams fat per sandwich*
*385 mg sodium per sandwich*
*23 mg cholesterol per sandwich*

**Substitutions:**
canned salmon, imitation crab

# OPEN-FACED CRAB MUFFINS

*Surimi seafood is a new fish product that has become available to consumers. Usually sold under a number of names, such as imitation crab meat or imitation lobster tail, surimi can be used in any recipe that calls for lobster or crab. It is currently made from Alaskan pollock, a mild white-fleshed fish, and flavored with real shellfish or shellfish extract and is fabricated into the shape, texture and color of shellfish. It can be a less expensive and still healthy alternative to the real thing!*

- ☐ ¾ cup low fat cottage cheese, blended
- ☐ ¼ cup Parmesan cheese
- ☐ ⅓ cup green onion, finely chopped
- ☐ 6 drops hot pepper sauce (Tabasco)
- ☐ 2 tsp. Worcestershire sauce
- ☐ 12 oz. imitation crab, shredded
- ☐ 6 English muffins (split in half) or substitute rice cakes

1. Mix blended cottage cheese, Parmesan cheese, green onion, Tabasco and Worcestershire sauce together in mixing bowl. Stir in imitation crab.
2. Spread ¼ cup crab mixture on each muffin half.
3. Place on cookie sheet and bake at 400° for 10-12 minutes. Serve for lunch with a salad. As an appetizer cut into triangles. **Makes 12 open-faced sandwiches.**

*112 calories per sandwich*
*1.4 grams fat per sandwich*
*303 mg sodium per sandwich*
*16 mg cholesterol per sandwich*

**Substitutions:**
crab, shrimp

# SHRIMP TOPPED RICE CAKES

*These are easy to heat in the microwave, too.*

- ☐ ¾ cup shrimp meat, cooked
- ☐ 3 ozs. light cream cheese, softened
- ☐ 2 T. fresh chives, chopped
- ☐ ⅛ tsp. hot pepper sauce (Tabasco)
- ☐ 8 plain rice cakes

1. Chop shrimp meat.
2. Combine cream cheese, chives and Tabasco in small bowl; beat at medium speed with electric mixer or in food processor until smooth. Stir in shrimp and blend mixture.
3. Spread the shrimp mixture evenly on rice cakes. Place rice cakes on baking sheet. Broil 5-6 inches from heat, 2 to 5 minutes or until warm. Serve immediately. **Makes 8 rice cake sandwiches.**

*73 calories per sandwich*
*2.3 grams fat per sandwich*
*105 mg sodium per sandwich*
*27 mg cholesterol per sandwich*

**Substitutions:**
imitation crab, lump crab meat

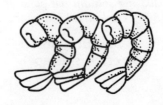

# HIGHLINER'S CHOICE SALMON CHOWDER

☐ 1 lb. salmon fillets, boneless and skinless

☐ 1 cup onion, chopped

☐ 1 cup potato, diced

☐ ¼ cup celery, chopped

☐ 1 T. polyunsaturated margarine

☐ 2 T. water

☐ 2 T. flour

☐ ¼ tsp. white pepper

☐ ¼ tsp. dried dill weed

☐ 1 can (8 oz.) stewed tomatoes

☐ 2 cans (13 oz. each) evaporated skim milk

☐ 1 cup part-skim Mozarella cheese, grated

☐ 2 T. parsley, chopped

1. Cut salmon into 1-inch pieces; set aside.
2. In saucepan saute onion, potato and celery in margarine and water until potatoes are tender.
3. Blend in flour, add pepper, dill, tomatoes, milk and salmon. Heat until soup thickens and comes to a simmer; stir occasionally. Simmer until salmon flakes when tested with fork.
4. Stir in cheese; add parsley. Serve with whole wheat roll. **Makes 4-6 servings.**

*362 calories per serving*
*11 grams fat per serving*
*452 mg sodium per serving*
*69 mg cholesterol per serving*

**Substitutions:**
scallops, crab meat, shrimp meat

# MANHATTAN SHELLFISH CHOWDER

- ☐ 1 medium onion, chopped
- ☐ 2 cloves garlic, minced
- ☐ 1 T. olive oil
- ☐ 1 can (10 oz.) low salt chicken broth
- ☐ ½ cup water
- ☐ 1 can (8 oz.) tomatoes
- ☐ 1 cup dry white wine
- ☐ 2 tsp. dried thyme
- ☐ 2 tsp. dried basil
- ☐ Pepper to taste
- ☐ 24 small or 12 medium clams, scrubbed
- ☐ ½ lb. sea scallops

1. In 8-quart saucepan over medium heat, saute onion and garlic in olive oil until tender.
2. Stir in chicken broth, water, tomatoes, wine and herbs; season with pepper. Simmer 10 minutes.
3. Increase heat to high; add clams and cook 2 minutes or until their shells open. Add scallops; cook until just done; about 2 minutes. Serve with whole wheat roll and green salad. **Makes 4 servings.**

*218 calories per serving*
*5.0 grams fat per serving*
*482 mg sodium per serving*
*203 mg cholesterol per serving*

### Substitutions:
chopped clams, squid or mussels
boneless, skinless, and chunked firm white-fleshed fish

# NORWEGIAN CRAB BISQUE

- ☐ 2 cups water
- ☐ 1 small onion, diced
- ☐ 2 stalks celery, chopped
- ☐ 2 medium potatoes, diced
- ☐ 2 carrots, sliced
- ☐ 1 cup frozen peas
- ☐ 6-8 whole allspice
- ☐ 1 tsp. dried dill weed

- ☐ ½ tsp. white pepper
- ☐ 2 cans (13 oz. each) evaporated skim milk
- ☐ 1 lb. imitation crab
- ☐ 1 T. parsley
- ☐ Dash of hot pepper sauce (Tabasco)

1. Place water, onions, celery, potatoes, carrots, peas, allspice, dill and white pepper in 4-quart saucepan. Bring to boil; reduce heat and simmer for 15 minutes. Remove and discard allspice.
2. Add milk and simmer (do not boil). Gently stir in imitation crab. Garnish with parsley and Tabasco. Serve with french bread. **Makes 6 servings.**

*229 calories per serving*
*0.3 gram fat per serving*
*629 mg sodium per serving*
*38 mg cholesterol per serving*

**Substitutions:**
scallops, shrimp, boneless, skinless, firm white-fleshed fish

# BOURBON STREET GUMBO

*Okra has a sticky, "gummy" consistency and acts as a thickener in soup, stews and chowders, hence the word "gumbo"!*

- ☐ ¼ cup polyunsaturated oil
- ☐ 1 white onion, chopped
- ☐ 2 stalks celery, chopped
- ☐ 4 cloves garlic, minced
- ☐ ½ green pepper, chopped
- ☐ 1 can (8 oz.) tomato sauce
- ☐ 1 can (16 oz.) whole tomaoes, mashed

- ☐ 2 cups water
- ☐ 2 pkgs. (8 oz. each) frozen okra, cut up
- ☐ 2 bay leaves
- ☐ Pepper to taste
- ☐ 1 lb. raw shrimp, peeled and deveined
- ☐ 1 lb. crab meat
- ☐ 1 T. dried parsley

1. Heat oil in kettle. Add onion, celery, garlic and green pepper and saute over medium heat until vegetables are tender-crisp.
2. Add tomato sauce and mashed tomatoes and simmer for 5 minutes.
3. Add water, okra, bay leaves and pepper. Cover and cook until okra is tender. Discard bay leaf. At this point gumbo base can be refrigerated or frozen.
4. To complete, reheat gumbo base, add shrimp and cook until shrimp turn opaque. Add crab meat; warm through. Garnish with parsley. **Makes 6-8 servings.**

*225 calories per serving*
*8.0 grams fat per serving*
*536 mg sodium per serving*
*140 mg cholesterol per serving*

**Substitutions:**
lobster meat, chopped squid, chopped clams

# ENTREES

# FISH

# ENTREES: FISH

# WHEN IS FISH COOKED?

Perfectly cooked fish is moist and has a delicate flavor. There's no secret about cooking fish properly. Fish is done when the flesh has just begun to turn from translucent to opaque (or white) and is firm but still moist. It should flake when tested with a fork.

## THE 10-MINUTE RULE FOR FISH

The 10-Minute Rule is one way to cook fish by conventional methods (but not deep-frying or microwaving). It can be used for baking (at 400° to 450°), grilling, broiling, poaching, steaming and sauteing. Here is how to use the 10-Minute Rule:

- Measure the fish at its thickest point. If the fish is stuffed or rolled, measure it after stuffing or rolling.

- Cook fish about 10 minutes per inch, turning it halfway through the cooking time. For example, a 1-inch fish steak should be cooked 5 minutes on each side for a total of 10 minutes. Pieces less than ½ inch thick do not have to be turned over. Test for doneness. Flake with a fork. Fish should reach an internal temperature of 145°.

- Add 5 minutes to the total cooking time for fish cooked in foil or in sauce.

- Double the cooking time for frozen fish that has not been defrosted. Use this rule as a general guideline since fillets often don't have uniform thickness.

# SEAFOOD ON THE RUN

Many of us live with a hectic schedule, fix several different meals for our families and feel too often that family members are just ships passing in the night. Seafood offers an easy and quick meal choice. It is a great convenience food. Consider a last minute meal from the supermarket. Try a stir-fry, such as "Country Garden Saute," page 71, with a seafood selection from the seafood counter and vegetables from the salad bar. It's easy to purchase shrimp, scallops or halibut and pre-cut vegetables with choices that could include mushrooms, celery, carrots, broccoli or onions.

Stopping at the seafood counter 3-4 times a week can be inconvenient. But frozen seafood is excellent and always on hand for a last minute meal. Purchase frozen seafood from your seafood merchant and keep it at 0°F to -20°F. Stock up on seafood that your local supermarket or seafood store has on sale. Thaw seafood in the refrigerator, under cold running water or in the microwave. Seafood can also be cooked from the frozen state by steaming, poaching, microwaving or baking, just double the cooking time. More "frozen-at-sea" products are appearing on the market so watch for that label.

Canned seafood products are also excellent for quick and easy to fix casseroles, salads and sandwiches. Keep a can in the refrigerator, cooled and ready to serve.

Eating seafood for the health, convenience, and taste of it is fun and easy. Enjoy to your heart's content!

Suggested recipes: Country Garden Saute, page 71
Four-Minute Flounder, page 110
Garlic Shrimp, page 122
Slender Steamed Sole, page 83

# BLUEFISH DIJON

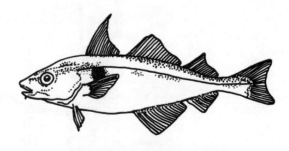

*Any type of fish is a healthier choice than the leanest red meat or poultry. Not only is fish low in cholesterol and saturated fat, but it's also high in omega-3 fatty acids, which may help lower cholesterol in the blood.*

☐ **3 T. Dijon mustard**

☐ **⅓ cup low fat yogurt**

☐ **2 lbs. bluefish**

☐ **Pepper to taste**

☐ **⅓ cup vermouth or dry white wine**

1. Combine mustard with yogurt in bowl; set aside.
2. Place fish in baking dish, season with pepper; spread fish with mustard mixture. Pour the vermouth or wine around fish.
3. Bake uncovered at 400°, until fish flakes when tested with fork. **Makes 8 servings.**

*153 calories per serving*
*5.2 grams fat per serving*
*147 mg sodium per serving*
*66 mg cholesterol per serving*

**Substitutions:**
halibut, Pacific rockfish (snapper), lingcod

# OCEAN COD SUPREME

☐ 1½ lbs. cod
☐ 1 cup dry white wine
(omit if desired)
☐ ¼ cup seasoned
bread crumbs

☐ 1 cup low fat yogurt
☐ ¼ cup green onion,
minced
☐ Paprika

1. Place fish in baking dish. Pour wine over cod and marinate in refrigerator 15-30 minutes.
2. Discard wine and pat fish dry with paper towels; dip both sides in bread crumbs. Place fish back in baking dish.
3. Combine yogurt and green onion and spread over fish. Sprinkle with paprika.
4. Bake in 400° oven about 15-20 minutes or until fish flakes when tested with fork. Serve with baked potatoes and steamed carrots. **Makes 6 servings.**

*152 calories per serving*
*1.5 grams fat per serving*
*132 mg sodium per serving*
*47 mg cholesterol per serving*

**Substitutions:**
Pacific rockfish (snapper), orange roughy, bluefish

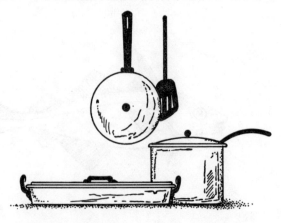

# COUNTRY GARDEN SAUTE

*Super salad bar dinner*

A once-a-week stir-fry is a good way to use up the bits and pieces of vegetables in the produce drawer and to vary them with the season. It's a great way to stretch a pound of seafood.

☐ 1 lb. firm fish, such as halibut

☐ Pepper

☐ 1 T. polyunsaturated oil or olive oil

☐ 1 cup carrots, sliced

☐ 1 cup celery, sliced

☐ 1 cup green onion, diagonally sliced

☐ 1 cup broccoli flowerets

☐ 1 cup mushrooms, sliced

☐ ¼ cup water

☐ ¼ cup chicken broth (low salt chicken broth may be used)

☐ 2 tsp. cornstarch

☐ ¼ tsp. fresh ginger, grated or ⅛ tsp. ground ginger

☐ 1 tsp. lemon peel

1. Remove bones and skin from fish; cut into 1-inch cubes. Season with pepper. Set aside.
2. In wok or frying pan, heat oil over medium-high heat. Add vegetables and water; saute until tender-crisp.
3. Add fish to pan. Combine stock, cornstarch, ginger and lemon peel; add to fish and vegetables.
4. Cook and stir until thickened and fish flakes when tested with fork. Serve with steamed rice. **Makes 4 servings.**

*186 calories per serving*
*5.0 grams fat per serving*
*155 mg sodium per serving*
*67 mg cholesterol per serving*

**Substitutions:**
shark, albacore tuna, salmon, prawns

# CUCUMBER HADDOCK

- ☐ 2 cups water
- ☐ 1 chicken-flavored bouillon cube (or eliminate water and add 2 cups low salt chicken broth)
- ☐ ⅛ t. garlic powder
- ☐ 2 medium cucumbers, unpeeled

- ☐ 1 lb. haddock
- ☐ 1 cup plain low fat yogurt
- ☐ 1½ tsp. lemon juice
- ☐ 2 T. cornstarch
- ☐ ½ tsp. dried dill weed

1. In skillet, dissolve bouillon in 2 cups boiling water. Add garlic powder and reduce to medium heat.
2. With tip of vegetable peeler score cucumbers lengthwise all around and cut in half lengthwise. Remove seeds and cut crosswise in ¼-inch slices.
3. Add prepared cucumbers and fish to broth and poach 5 minutes until fish flakes when tested with fork.
4. Remove and drain cucumbers and fish with slotted spoon and place on serving dish.
5. In bowl, combine remaining ingredients and add to broth in skillet. Simmer until sauce thickens; pour over fish and cucumbers. **Makes 4 servings.**

*134 calories per serving*
*1.5 grams fat per serving*
*350 mg sodium per serving*
*70 mg cholesterol per serving*

**Substitutions:**
salmon, halibut, orange roughy

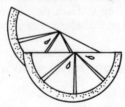

# CASEROLE DELIGHT

*Water chestnuts, commonly used in Chinese cuisine, are not nuts but tubers. Unlike nuts, they are low in calories (about 14 calories per ounce or approximately four water chestnuts) and almost fat-free. Great for a crunch in salads, sandwiches and stir-fry.*

- ☐ 1 cup dry vermouth
- ☐ 1½ lbs. cooked halibut, flaked
- ☐ 1 tsp. Italian Seafood Seasoning (see page 138)
- ☐ 1 large onion, chopped
- ☐ 2 cups celery, sliced
- ☐ 1 cup unsweetened pineapple chunks, drained

- ☐ 1 can (8 oz.) sliced water chestnuts
- ☐ 1 cup low fat cottage cheese, blended
- ☐ ¼ cup slivered almonds, chopped
- ☐ 1 cup part-skim Mozzarella cheese, grated
- ☐ ¼ cup chow mein noodles

1. Pour vermouth over fish in 1½-quart casserole dish. Cover and marinate for 15 minutes.
2. Drain fish. Sprinkle Italian Seafood Seasoning over fish.
3. Stir in onions, celery, pineapple chunks, chestnuts, and blended cottage cheese.
4. Sprinkle almonds, Mozzarella cheese and chow mein noodles over the top.
5. Bake at 375° for 25 minutes. Serve with rice. **Makes 6-8 servings.**

*294 calories per serving*
*9.0 grams fat per serving*
*293 mg sodium per serving*
*61 mg cholesterol per serving*

**Substitutions:**
canned salmon, canned tuna

# BEST DRESSED MACKEREL OR TROUT

☐ 2 lbs. dressed, whole
  mackerel or trout

☐ Pepper

☐ 1 T. polyunsaturated
  margarine

☐ Lemon juice

☐ 1 onion, thinly sliced

1. Pepper inside and outside of fish. Put dabs of margarine and squeeze lemon juice inside body cavity. Place onions inside of fish. Wrap in foil.

2. Bake in 400° oven or place on rack in large pot over 2-3 inches of boiling water to steam. Cooking time is 10 minutes per pound, or about 20 minutes. Cook until fish flakes when tested with fork. Serve with steamed or boiled potatoes and green salad. **Makes 8 servings.**

*WITH MACKEREL:*
*200 calories per serving*
*9.6 grams fat per serving*
*110 mg sodium per serving*
*45 mg cholesterol per serving*

*WITH TROUT:*
*235 calories per serving*
*13.7 grams fat per serving*
*82 mg sodium per serving*
*55 mg cholesterol per serving*

**Substitutions:**
any variety and size of whole, dressed fish,
whole, dressed salmon

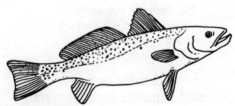

# MONKFISH SAUTE

*Monkfish was named in the Mediterranean Sea region. This large, ugly fish was discarded by fishermen as scrapfish, but the monks found them to be quite tasty. So came the name "monksfish". Monkfish is best prepared by cutting into thin slices. At full thickness, by steaming or baking. Poaching monkfish is also excellent.*

- □ 1 pkg. (6 oz.) frozen pea pods
- □ 1½ T. olive oil
- □ 2 lbs. monkfish, cut into ½-inch slices
- □ 2 tomatoes, cut into eighths
- □ ¼ cup water
- □ 2 T. cornstarch
- □ 2 T. light soy sauce
- □ ⅛ t. pepper

1. Thaw and drain pea pods; set aside.
2. Heat olive oil in large skillet. Add monkfish and cook over medium heat for 2 minutes, stirring frequently. Add pea pods and tomatoes.
3. Combine water, cornstarch, soy sauce and pepper in small bowl.
4. Add to monkfish mixture and cook until sauce is thick and seafood is opaque, stirring frequently. Serve over steamed rice. **Makes 8 servings.**

*138 calories per serving*
*4.0 grams fat per serving*
*374 mg sodium per serving*
*95 mg cholesterol per serving*

**Substitutions:**
scallops, squid rings, halibut cheeks

# ORANGE ROUGHY WITH TOMATO-TARRAGON SAUCE

## POACHED FISH:

- ☐ 1 small carrot, finely diced
- ☐ 1 small rib celery, finely diced
- ☐ 1 small onion, finely diced
- ☐ 1 can (10 oz.) low salt chicken broth
- ☐ 4 cups water

- ☐ 3 sprigs parsley
- ☐ 1 clove garlic, minced
- ☐ ½ tsp. whole black pepper
- ☐ ½ tsp. dried red pepper, crushed
- ☐ 1 lb. orange roughy

## TOMATO-TARRAGON SAUCE:

- ☐ 1 T. polyunsaturated margarine
- ☐ 4 tsp. flour
- ☐ 1 cup reserved poaching liquid

- ☐ ¼ tsp. dried tarragon, crushed
- ☐ Pepper to taste
- ☐ 2 tomatoes, diced
- ☐ 2 tsp. parsley, chopped

1. To prepare poaching liquid: combine carrot, celery, onion, chicken broth, water, parsley, garlic, whole pepper and red pepper in large saucepan or poacher. Place on top of burner, bring to boil; reduce heat and simmer for 20 minutes.

2. Bring the liquid back to boil and immerse the fillets. Reduce the heat and simmer for 5-10 minutes or until fish flakes when tested with fork.

3. While fish is poaching, prepare sauce. In saucepan, heat margarine until melted, add flour and cook until bubbly, about 1 minute. Whisk in 1 cup hot poaching liquid, tarragon, pepper and tomatoes. Simmer for 5 minutes.

4. Place each serving of fish on plate and top with sauce. Garnish with parsley. **Makes 4 servings.**

*137 calories per serving*
*3.6 grams fat per serving*
*145 mg sodium per serving*
*78 mg cholesterol per serving*

**Substitutions:**
ocean perch, cod, sea bass

# CHEESEY ROCKFISH (SNAPPER)

- ☐ 2 T. polyunsaturated margarine, melted
- ☐ ½ cup Parmesan cheese
- ☐ ¼ cup yellow cornmeal
- ☐ ¼ cup flour
- ☐ ½ tsp. pepper
- ☐ 1 tsp. Spanish paprika
- ☐ 2 lbs. Pacific rockfish (snapper), skinless and boneless

1. Pour melted margarine into baking pan.
2. Combine Parmesan cheese, cornmeal, flour, pepper and paprika together in paper bag. Place fish in bag and shake to coat each fillet.
3. Place fish in baking dish. Turn fish once to coat with margarine. Pour remaining cheese/cornmeal/flour mixture onto fish.
4. Bake at 400° until golden brown and fish flakes when tested with fork, approximately 15-20 minutes. Serve with bulgur and steamed vegetables. **Makes 8 servings.**

*188 calories per serving*
*5.5 grams fat per serving*
*184 mg sodium per serving*
*392 mg cholesterol per serving*

**Substitutions:**
bluefish, ocean perch, cod

# POACHED SABLEFISH (BLACK COD)

- ☐ 8 cups water
- ☐ 2 T. light soy sauce
- ☐ 2 stalks green onions, chopped
- ☐ 1 clove garlic, chopped
- ☐ Juice of ½ lemon
- ☐ 1 lb. sablefish (black cod), fillets or steaks

1. Bring water to boil in 8-quart sauce pan. Add soy sauce, green onions, garlic and lemon juice and simmer for 20 minutes.
2. Place sablefish in poaching liquid. Simmer for 8-10 minutes or until fish flakes when tested with fork. **Makes 4 servings.**

*162 calories per serving*
*7.5 grams fat per serving*
*457 mg sodium per serving*
*73 mg cholesterol per serving*

**Substitutions:**
bluefish, cod, salmon

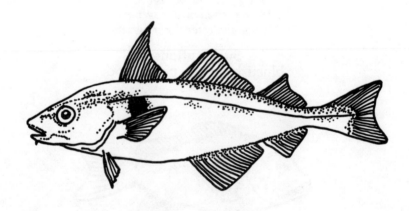

# BRISTOL BAY SALMON

*Elegant entertaining idea*

- ☐ 1½ lbs. salmon fillets or steaks
- ☐ ½ cup low fat yogurt
- ☐ 1 T. mayonnaise
- ☐ 2 T. onion, minced
- ☐ 1 tsp. dried basil

1. Place salmon in baking pan.
2. Mix remaining ingredients together and spread over salmon.
3. Bake in 400⁰ oven for 10-15 minutes or until salmon flakes when tested with fork. Serve with boiled new potatoes and vegetables. **Makes 6 servings.**

*188 calories per serving*
*10.0 grams fat per serving*
*104 mg sodium per serving*
*75 mg cholesterol per serving*

**Substitutions:**
halibut, spearfish, swordfish

 *KNOW YOUR SALMON!*

**KING SALMON:** also known as Chinook. Largest of all salmon with the record being 168 lbs. Color ranges from white to deep red and very high in oil content. Flavorful.

**SOCKEYE SALMON:** also known as red or blueback. Averages 6 lbs., deep red color and high oil content. Flavorful.

**SILVER SALMON:** also known as coho. Averages 4-12 lbs. Flesh is orange-red in color and oil content is fairly high.

**PINK SALMON:** also known as humpback or humpie because it develops a hump before spawning. Average weight is 3-8 lbs. Light colored flesh, less oil and very delicate flavor.

**CHUM SALMON:** also called keta, silverbrite or dog salmon. Weighs 8-10 lbs. Typically the last salmon up the river at the end of summer and into late fall. Dubbed dog salmon because it was fed to dogs when salmon was more abundant. Firm flesh which tends to be pale.

# THAI-STYLE SALMON POTATO

□ ½ cup onion, chopped

□ 1 T. fresh ginger root, slivered

□ ¼ to ½ tsp. red pepper, crushed

□ 1 T. polyunsaturated oil

□ 1 lb. salmon, skinned, boned and cubed

□ 2 cups broccoli flowerets

□ 1 cup pea pods

□ 1 cup tofu cubes

□ 1 cup cucumber, vertically sliced

□ 2 shiitake mushrooms, rehydrated & thinly sliced

□ ¾ cup water

□ ¼ cup vinegar

□ 4 tsp. packed brown sugar

□ 1 T. cornstarch

□ 1 tsp. lemon peel, grated

□ Pepper to taste

□ 4 large Russet potatoes, baked

1. Saute onion, ginger root and red pepper in oil until onion is tender; add salmon and cook 3 minutes.

2. Add broccoli, pea pods, tofu, cucumber and mushrooms; cook until vegetables are tender-crisp.

3. Combine water, vinegar, brown sugar, cornstarch, lemon peel and pepper; stir into vegetables. Cook until mixture thickens and boils.

4. To serve, split baked potatoes lengthwise and open by gently squeezing from the bottom. Spoon ¼ of salmon mixture over each potato. **Makes 4 servings.**

*462 calories per serving*
*14.0 grams fat per serving*
*81 mg sodium per serving*
*72 mg cholesterol per serving*

## Substitutions:
canned salmon, canned, water-packed tuna

# CURRIED SALMON

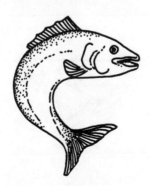 *This recipe is especially good with milder salmon varieties such as chum, coho or pinks.*

- ☐ 1 cup white wine
- ☐ 4 green onions, diagonally cut
- ☐ 1 bay leaf
- ☐ 1 T. polyunsaturated margarine

- ☐ 1-2 tsp. curry powder
- ☐ 2 ripe pears or apples, cored and sliced
- ☐ 1 red pepper, julienne cut
- ☐ 1½ lbs. salmon fillets

1. In large, deep skillet combine wine, green onions, bay leaf, margarine and curry powder. Heat to boil.
2. Add fruit and vegetables and simmer about 5-10 minutes or until tender-crisp. Remove fruit and vegetables onto serving platter and keep warm in oven. Discard bay leaf.
3. Add salmon to liquid in skillet and cover. Steam until fish flakes when tested with fork.
4. Place fish on serving platter over vegetables and fruit. Drizzle any remaining liquid over all. **Makes 4-6 servings.**

*258 calories per serving*
*9.7 grams fat per serving*
*100 mg sodium per serving*
*75 mg cholesterol per serving*

**Substitutions:**
trout, black cod, scallops

# SAVORY SALMON LOAF
*Fisherman's Favorite*

- ☐ 1 can (15½ oz.) salmon
- ☐ 3 slices bread, torn into small pieces
- ☐ ⅓ cup onion, finely minced
- ☐ ¼ cup skim milk
- ☐ 2 eggs
- ☐ 2 T. parsley, minced
- ☐ 1 T. lemon juice
- ☐ ¼ tsp. dried dill weed
- ☐ Dash pepper

1. Drain salmon, reserving 2 T. liquid; flake.
2. Combine all ingredients including reserved salmon liquid. Place in lightly-oiled loaf pan.
3. Bake at 350⁰ for 45 minutes. Serve with steamed vegetables.

## ALTERNATE PREPARATION METHOD — SALMON PATTIES
1. Prepare salmon mixture as above, omitting milk.
2. Shape into 8 patties.
3. Saute in pan with 1 T. polyunsaturated oil until golden brown. Serve on hamburger buns with favorite garnishes. **Makes 6 servings.**

*193 calories per serving*
*7.8 grams fat per serving*
*388 mg sodium per serving*
*98 mg cholesterol per serving*

**Substitutions:**
leftover, cooked, flaked trout, salmon or halibut

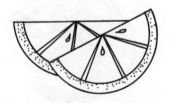

# SLENDER STEAMED SOLE

### SAUCE:

□ 1 T. light soy sauce

□ 2 tsp. polyunsaturated oil

□ 1 tsp. fresh ginger, finely chopped

□ 1 lb. sole fillets

1. To prepare sauce: in mixing bowl combine soy sauce, oil and chopped ginger root.
2. Arrange fish on steaming rack. Brush fish with sauce.
3. Place rack over boiling water. Cover and steam 7-10 minutes or until fish flakes when tested with fork. Serve with steamed rice and vegetables. **Makes 4 servings.**

*102 calories per serving*
*1.8 grams fat per serving*
*260 mg sodium per serving*
*51 mg cholesterol per serving*

**Substitutions:**
orange roughy, cod, tilefish

# HEARTFELT SOLE

☐ 1 T. olive oil
☐ 3 shallots, minced
☐ 1 clove garlic, minced
☐ ¼ to ¾ cup white wine

☐ 1½ lbs. sole fillet
☐ ¼ tsp. dried dill weed
☐ Pepper to taste
☐ Parsley
☐ Lemon slices

1. In saute pan heat oil. Add shallots and garlic; saute for 1 minute. Add wine and heat to boiling.

2. Add sole to pan and sprinkle with dill weed. Spoon shallot and liquid over sole. Simmer 2-3 minutes or until fish flakes when tested with fork. Not necessary to turn fish. Pepper to taste.

3. Remove fish to warm serving plate. Turn pan to high heat and reduce juice. Spoon juice over sole fillets. Garnish with parsley and lemon slice. **Makes 6 servings.**

*120 calories per serving*
*3.0 grams fat per serving*
*62 mg sodium per serving*
*50 mg cholesterol per serving*

**Substitutions:**
pollock, orange roughy, flounder

# COLUMBIA RIVER STURGEON

*Sturgeon is famed for its caviar, but the meat is highly prized by the locals along the Columbia River, located between the states of Oregon and Washington.*

□ 1 T. fresh ginger root, sliced
□ 1 tsp. pepper
□ ½ cup fresh cilantro leaves
□ 1 clove garlic

□ 1 T. light soy sauce
□ 2 T. olive oil
□ Juice and rind of 2 lemons
□ 1½ lbs. sturgeon steaks

1. Combine ginger root, pepper, cilantro, garlic, soy sauce, olive oil, lemon juice and lemon rind in food processor or blender and puree. Allow flavors to blend 15 minutes.
2. Place fish steaks in shallow glass dish and cover with marinade, turning fish several times to coat evenly.
3. Broil or barbecue fish, allowing ten minutes of cooking time for each inch of thickness. Baste periodically with marinade. Serve immediately. **Makes 6 servings.**

*166 calories per serving*
*9.2 grams fat per serving*
*N/A mg sodium per serving*
*N/A mg cholesterol per serving*

**Substitutions:**
swordfish, shark, lingcod

# GRILLED SWORDFISH WITH HERBS

♥ *Swordfish: This firm-flesh fish with a fine grain has a distinctive flavor and can have flesh that is anywhere from white to light tan or pink. It usually is sold as steaks. The flesh tends to be dry if not basted often during cooking; use a basting sauce made with lemon juice, olive oil and herbs. Baste before broiling or baking, and use the marinade to baste the fish during cooking.*

☐ 1 T. olive oil
☐ 2 T. lime juice
☐ ½ cup Chardonnay wine
☐ 1 T. dry mustard
☐ 1 tsp. mustard seeds

☐ 1 T. chili powder
☐ 1 tsp. pepper
☐ 2 T. dried cilantro or 4 T. fresh cilantro, finely chopped
☐ 1 lb. swordfish steaks

1. Combine olive oil, lime juice and Chardonnay in bowl. Add spices.
2. Pour marinade over swordfish steaks and marinate for 15-20 minutes.
3. Grill swordfish over hot coals, about 5 minutes per side, or until fish turns opaque. Baste with marinade while cooking. **Makes 4 servings.**

*243 calories per serving*
*8.5 grams fat per serving*
*79 mg sodium per serving*
*56 mg cholesterol per serving*

**Substitutions:**
marlin, halibut, cod

# SZECHWAN STIR FRY

*Tuna: Depending on the species, the flesh will range from dark pink to red but will turn white to gray-white when cooked.*

## SZECHWAN SAUCE:

☐ 2 T. rice vinegar

☐ 1½ T. light soy sauce

☐ 1 tsp. sesame oil

☐ ½ tsp. dried red pepper flakes

## STIR FRY:

☐ 1 lb. albacore tuna, cut in 1-inch chunks

☐ 1 T. polyunsaturated oil

☐ 2 tsp. fresh ginger, peeled and minced

☐ 1 clove garlic, peeled and minced

☐ ¼ cup water

☐ 1 cup broccoli flowerets

☐ 1 cup carrots, thinly sliced

☐ ½ small red pepper, coarsely chopped

☐ ½ cup bamboo shoots, sliced

☐ ½ cup water chestnuts, sliced

☐ 1 cup snow peas

☐ 3 T. green onion, thinly sliced

1. To make Szechwan sauce: combine sauce ingredients in bowl. Add tuna to bowl to marinate.
2. Heat oil in wok over medium heat. Add ginger, garlic and water and saute for 30 seconds. Add broccoli and carrots to pan and stir fry for 3 minutes. Add red pepper, bamboo shoots, water chestnuts and snow peas; cover and simmer for 4 minutes.
3. Add marinated tuna, Szechwan sauce and green onion to wok and stir.
4. Saute 3-6 minutes or until tuna flakes when tested with fork. Serve immediately with steamed rice. **Makes 6 servings.**

*158 calories per serving*
*5.5 grams fat per serving*
*244 mg sodium per serving*
*14 mg cholesterol per serving*

**Substitutions:**
mahi mahi, squid rings, shrimp or prawns

# SAUCY TUNA FOR FOUR

## WHITE SAUCE:
- ☐ 1 T. polyunsaturated margarine
- ☐ 1 T. flour
- ☐ 1 can (13 oz.) evaporated skim milk

## CASSEROLE:
- ☐ 1 can (4 oz.) sliced mushrooms, drained
- ☐ 2 T. onion, minced
- ☐ 1 T. pimiento, chopped
- ☐ ¼ tsp. dried dill weed
- ☐ 1 T. lemon juice
- ☐ 1 cup frozen peas
- ☐ 1 can (6½ oz.) water-packed tuna, drained
- ☐ 1 pkg. (10 oz.) frozen broccoli spears, cooked & drained
- ☐ 2 T. Parmesan cheese

1. Prepare white sauce: melt margarine and blend in flour over medium heat in 4-quart saucepan. Add milk slowly while stirring.
2. Boil one minute, stirring until smooth.
3. Add remaining ingredients except broccoli spears and Parmesan cheese.
4. Lay broccoli spears in au grautin dishes and pour tuna sauce over broccoli and sprinkle with Parmesan cheese.
5. Bake uncovered at 350° for 20 minutes. Serve with green salad and whole wheat roll. **Makes 4 servings.**

*243 calories per serving*
*4.3 grams fat per serving*
*539 mg sodium per serving*
*17 mg cholesterol per serving*

**Substitutions:**
canned salmon, shrimp, peeled and deveined

# ENTREES

# SHELLFISH

## CHAPTER 6
# ENTREES: SHELLFISH

# WHEN IS SHELLFISH COOKED?

Shellfish, like fish, should not be overcooked. If it's cooked too long, it becomes tough and dry and loses much of its fine flavor.

Some shellfish and all surimi seafood are already cooked when purchased. Merely heat them for a few minutes until they are uniformly heated.

Cook raw shellfish, shucked or in the shell, very lightly. You can actually see when shellfish is cooked:

- Raw shrimp turn pink and firm. Cooking time depends on the size. It takes from 3 to 5 minutes to boil or steam 1 pound of medium-size shrimp in the shell.

- Shucked shellfish (oysters, clams and mussels) become plump and opaque. The edges of oysters start to curl. Overcooking causes them to shrink and toughen.

- Oysters, clams and mussels, in the shell, open. Remove them one-by-one as they open and continue cooking until all are done.

- Scallops turn milky-white or opaque and firm. Sea scallops take 3 to 4 minutes to cook through; the smaller bay scallops take 30 to 60 seconds.

- Boiled lobster turns bright red. Allow 18 to 20 minutes per pound, starting from the time the water comes back to the boil. Broiled split lobster takes about 15 minutes.

- Cooking time for crabs depends on the type and preparation method. Sauteed or deep-fried soft-shell crabs take about 3 minutes each. Steamed hard-shell blue crabs or rock crabs take about 25 to 30 minutes for a large pot of them.

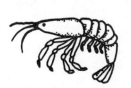

# MOTHER'S OYSTER PIE

- ☐ ¾ cup seasoned bread crumbs
- ☐ 1 can (17 oz.) creamed corn
- ☐ Pepper to taste

- ☐ 2 jars (8 oz. each) small, whole oysters with liquid
- ☐ 1 jar (2 oz.) pimiento, chopped
- ☐ 4 tsp. polyunsaturated margarine

1. Divide equally into the bottom of 4 au grautin baking dishes the following: 6 tablespoons bread crumbs, ½ can corn, pepper, and 1 jar of oysters.
2. Repeat layers. Top with remaining bread crumbs and pimiento. Dot with margarine.
3. Bake at 400⁰ for 20 minutes. **Makes 4 servings.**

*210 calories per serving*
*6.5 grams fat per serving*
*550 mg sodium per serving*
*56 mg cholesterol per serving*

# ROMANTIC SCALLOPS FOR TWO

 *Olive oils range in smell and taste from light and subtly fruity to unpleasantly strong. So try different brands. Many health professionals now recommend it for all-purpose use, spawning a new product, "extra light" olive oil, which has little taste.*

- ☐ ½ lb. sea scallops
- ☐ Skim milk
- ☐ 2 T. flour
- ☐ 1 T. olive oil
- ☐ ¼ cup wine
- ☐ ¼ cup shallots, chopped
- ☐ 2 T. green onion, chopped
- ☐ 2 tsp. dried parsley
- ☐ 1 lemon
- ☐ Lemon pepper to taste

1. Flatten scallops with a cleaver and dip in milk and flour.
2. Saute scallops in a saucepan with olive oil.
3. Remove scallops from pan and deglaze pan with white wine. Add shallots, green onion and chopped parsley. Simmer and pour over scallops. Squeeze lemon over scallops and season with lemon pepper. **Makes 2 servings.**

*200 calories per serving*
*5.7 grams fat per serving*
*245 mg sodium per serving*
*55 mg cholesterol per serving*

**Substitutions:**
oysters, monkfish medallions

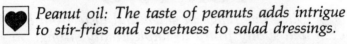

# PRAWN AND SCALLOP SAUTE

*Peanut oil: The taste of peanuts adds intrigue to stir-fries and sweetness to salad dressings.*

- ☐ 2 T. peanut oil
- ☐ 1 T. sesame seeds
- ☐ 1 clove garlic, minced
- ☐ Juice of half lemon
- ☐ ¼ lb. sugar peas
- ☐ ½ cup green onion, finely chopped
- ☐ ½ red pepper, seeded and chopped
- ☐ 1 cup mushrooms, sliced
- ☐ ½ tsp. dried basil
- ☐ 1 lb. small prawns, peeled and deveined
- ☐ ½ lb. sea scallops
- ☐ Pepper to taste

1. In large skillet, melt margarine; saute sesame seeds and garlic until lightly browned. Add lemon juice.

2. Add sugar peas, green onion, red pepper, mushrooms and basil; saute until tender-crisp.

3. Push vegetables aside and saute prawns and scallops until opaque. Pepper to taste. Serve with pasta and french bread. **Makes 6 servings.**

*175 calories per serving*
*5.2 grams fat per serving*
*209 mg sodium per serving*
*135 mg cholesterol per serving*

**Substitutions:**
albacore tuna, halibut, salmon

# SPICY POACHED SHRIMP (PRAWNS)

*Poaching is as easy as boiling water. It is also among the healthiest ways to prepare fish, since no fat is used when you cook; instead, you simmer the fish in a flavorful liquid for a moist and tasty meal every time.*

- ☐ 2 T. mustard seed
- ☐ 1 T. whole black pepper
- ☐ 1 tsp. Spanish paprika
- ☐ 1 tsp. garlic, minced

- ☐ ½ tsp. onion powder
- ☐ 4 cups water
- ☐ 1 lb. raw shrimp or prawns

1. Place mustard seed and whole black pepper in cheesecloth bag.
2. Place all spices, including spice bag, in water and bring to boil; reduce heat and simmer for 10 minutes.
3. Add shrimp or prawns and cook for 3 minutes or until shrimp/prawns turn opaque. Remove shrimp/prawns from water and rinse in cold water to stop cooking process. Chill. Serve with cocktail sauce as an appetizer or in salad. **Makes 4 servings.**

*90 calories per serving*
*0.8 gram fat per serving*
*140 mg sodium per serving*
*158 mg cholesterol per serving*

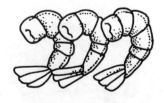

# ITALIAN FISHERMAN'S SPAGHETTI

♥ *About 99% of all shrimp you buy has been frozen. This does no harm to the nutritional value of the shrimp and it tastes as delicious as fresh.*

☐ 1 cup onion, chopped
☐ 2 cloves garlic, minced
☐ 1 T. olive oil
☐ 1 can (8 oz.) tomato sauce
☐ 1 can (28 oz.) whole tomatoes, undrained and mashed
☐ 1 tsp. each dried basil, thyme, marjoram and oregano

☐ 1 bay leaf
☐ ¼ tsp. pepper
☐ 1 T. parsley, minced
☐ 1 lb. raw medium shrimp, peeled and deveined

1. In large kettle, saute onion and garlic in oil until tender.
2. Add tomato sauce, tomatoes and spices. Let simmer 20-30 minutes, stirring occasionally. Remove and discard bay leaf.
3. Add shrimp; cover and simmer 3-5 minutes or until shrimp turns opaque. Stir occasionally. Serve over hot spaghetti. **Makes 6-8 servings.**

*106 calories per serving*
*2.2 grams fat per serving*
*375 mg sodium per serving*
*89 mg cholesterol per serving*

**Substitutions:**
clams, mussels, squid rings

# SHRIMP AND TOMATO TOSTADA

## SALSA:

- ☐ 2½ cups fresh tomatoes, chopped
- ☐ ½ cup green pepper, chopped
- ☐ ½ cup onion, minced
- ☐ 1 can (4 oz.) green chiles, diced
- ☐ 1 T. sugar

- ☐ ¾ tsp. cilantro (chopped) or coriander
- ☐ ½ tsp. dried whole oregano
- ☐ 2½ T. lemon or lime juice
- ☐ 1 can (8 oz.) tomato sauce

## TOSTADA:

- ☐ 3 cups water
- ☐ 1 lb. raw shrimp, unpeeled, medium size
- ☐ 8 tortillas (flour or corn)

- ☐ Suggested garnishes: shredded lettuce part-skim Mozzarella cheese, grated

1. Combine salsa ingredients in medium bowl; stir well. Cover mixture and let stand at room temperature for 1 hour.
2. Bring water to boil in saucepan; add shrimp, and cook 3 minutes or until shrimp turns opaque. Drain shrimp well, and rinse with cold water. Peel and devein shrimp.
3. Layer shredded lettuce and Mozzarella cheese on tortillas. Top with shrimp and salsa. Also excellent as a salad. **Makes 8 servings.**

*196 calories per tostada*
*2.5 grams fat per tostada*
*314 mg sodium per tostada*
*89 mg cholesterol per tostada*

**Substitutions:**
imitation crab, crayfish

# PHILIPPINE PANSIT

- ☐ 1 pkg. (6½ oz.) Maifun (rice sticks)
- ☐ 1 T. polyunsaturated oil
- ☐ 2 cups frozen peas
- ☐ 1 medium onion, sliced
- ☐ 1 cup mushrooms, sliced
- ☐ ½ cup carrots, grated
- ☐ 1 cup cabbage, shredded
- ☐ ¼ cup light soy sauce
- ☐ 1 cup chicken broth or low salt chicken broth
- ☐ ½ lb. cooked shrimp, peeled and deveined

1. Soak Maifun in hot water (enough to cover) until soft (about 10 minutes). Drain and cut into shorter lengths; set aside.
2. Heat oil in frying pan. Add peas, onion, mushrooms, carrots, cabbage, soy sauce and chicken broth. Mix and bring to full boil.
3. Lower heat, add shrimp and Maifun. Cook until Maifun is tender or until liquid is gone. **Makes 6-8 servings.**

*Made with low salt broth:*
*165 calories per serving*
*2.6 grams fat per serving*
*404 mg sodium per serving*
*33 mg cholesterol per serving*

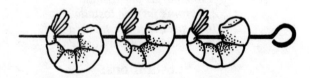

# SPINACH FETTUCINE WITH SHRIMP

☐ 2 ozs. dry spinach fettucine

☐ 1 tsp. cornstarch

☐ ½ cup orange juice

☐ 2 tsp. polyunsaturated margarine

☐ 4 large shrimp, peeled, deveined and sliced lengthwise in half

☐ ½ cup snow peas

☐ ¼ cup mushrooms, sliced

☐ ½ cup tomato, chopped

☐ 1 carrot, cut into curls

☐ Fresh chives for garnish

1. Cook fettucine according to package directions.

2. Meanwhile, blend cornstarch and orange juice together in small bowl until smooth; set aside.

3. In skillet, over high heat, melt margarine and add shrimp, snow peas, mushrooms and tomatoes and saute just until shrimp curl and become opaque, about 2 minutes.

4. Stir in orange sauce; cook until sauce thickens, about 1 minute. Remove from heat.

5. When pasta is almost done, toss in carrot curls, cook 1 minute longer and drain.

6. Toss with sauce and mushrooms and season with fresh black pepper; garnish with fresh chives. Serve with french bread. **Makes 2 servings.**

*268 calories per serving*
*7.0 grams fat per serving*
*124 mg sodium per serving*
*79 mg cholesterol per serving*

# SAUCY SQUID

☐ 12 large squid

### STUFFING:

☐ ⅓ cup uncooked brown rice     ☐ ½ tsp. garlic powder

☐ ½ cup celery, chopped     ☐ ½ tsp. cumin

☐ ½ cup onion, chopped     ☐ 2 cups water

### SAUCE:

☐ 1 can (28 oz.) tomatoes, undrained

☐ 2 T. lemon juice

☐ 1 green pepper, seeded and chopped

☐ 1 cup mushrooms, sliced

☐ 1 T. fresh dill weed, finely chopped or 1 tsp. dried dill weed

☐ ¼ tsp. saffron

☐ Reserved chopped squid, if desired

1. Clean squid, leaving mantles (bodies) whole for stuffing. The tentacles may be chopped and reserved for adding to sauce.

2. To make stuffing: place all stuffing ingredients in 2-quart sauce pan. Stir. Bring to boil, reduce heat and simmer for 40 minutes. If any liquid remains, drain off. Let the rice mixture cool for ease of handling in stuffing the squid.

3. To make sauce: combine all ingredients for sauce, stir and set aside.

4. Lightly stuff each squid mantle. The amount to use depends on the size of each squid. Do not overstuff as the squid tends to shrink as it cooks, while the rice may continue to swell. Reserve any extra stuffing. Close openings and secure with toothpicks.

5. Lay the stuffed squid in a single layer in a 8" x 11" x 2" casserole dish. Pour the sauce over squid. Place in 350° oven and bake 45 minutes. If there is extra stuffing, it may be reheated in the oven the last 15 minutes of baking time and served as a side dish with squid and sauce. **Makes 4-6 servings.**

*135 calories per serving*
*1.5 grams fat per serving*
*380 mg sodium per serving*
*230 mg cholesterol per serving*

# STUFFED SQUID SUPREME

☐ 12 large squid

## SAUCE:

☐ ½ cup onion, chopped
☐ 1 clove garlic, minced
☐ 2 T. olive oil
☐ 1 can (6 oz.) tomato paste
☐ ¾ cup water

☐ ¼ cup celery, chopped
☐ 1 T. oyster sauce
☐ ⅛ tsp. lemon pepper
☐ 3 bay leaves

## STUFFING:

☐ 16 oz. part-skim
   Ricotta cheese
☐ ¼ cup fresh parsley, chopped

☐ 3-4 cooked artichoke
   hearts, chopped

1. Clean squid, leaving mantles (bodies whole for stuffing. Remove tentacles from squid. Chop and reserve for stuffing.
2. Saute onion and garlic in oil until lightly browned. Add tomato paste and water. Add celery, oyster sauce, lemon pepper and bay leaves. Cover and simmer for 20 minutes, or until sauce is thick.
3. To make stuffing: combine Ricotta cheese, chopped tentacles, parsley and artichokes. Fill the squid with cheese stuffing (a pastry gun works well). Close openings and secure with toothpicks.
4. Place filled squid in large, 2-inch deep baking dish and pour sauce on top; remove bay leaves. Bake at 325° for 20-25 minutes. **Makes 4-6 servings.**

*296 calories per serving*
*12.0 grams fat per serving*
*270 mg sodium per serving*
*240 mg cholesterol per serving*

# MICROWAVE

## CHAPTER 7

# MICROWAVE

# MAKING WAVES

## SEAFOOD MICROWAVE TECHNIQUES

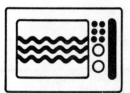

Seafood cooks perfectly in the microwave oven. It remains tender, moist and flavorful. Almost all kinds of seafood can be prepared in the microwave oven. However, there are many microwave ovens on the market and they vary in power. You may need to experiment to find the right cooking time for a particular recipe.

Watch closely when you try a new recipe for the first time. If a range of times is given, start with the shortest one. You can always put the dish back in the oven and cook it a little longer, but you cannot turn the clock back if it has cooked too long. Write the correct time down on the recipe for future reference.

Split-second timing is the secret to cooking seafood in the microwave. Seafood cooked by microwave is done when the flesh has just begun to change from translucent to opaque or white and when it is firm but still moist. Seafood will continue to cook after it has been removed from the microwave, so take the dish out before it looks done — when the outer edges are opaque with the center still slightly translucent. Allow the fish to stand, covered, for a few minutes before serving.

*Getting everyone to sit down to dinner at the same time is a rare feat. The solution: a meal of microwaved foods that will "hold" and remain at the ideal serving temperature. Holding time is the length of time a properly wrapped or covered food will stay hot after cooking is complete. It should not be confused with standing time, during which microwaved food is still cooking. Fish can be tented with foil or wrapped in plastic to retain heat. Whole fish (2-3 lbs.) will hold its serving temperature for 7 minutes; fish fillets (4 1-lb. fillets) will hold its temperature also for 7 minutes!*

## COOKING FISH IN THE MICROWAVE OVEN

- Use a shallow microwave-proof dish to hold the fish.
- Shield the head and tail of a whole fish with aluminum foil to guard against excess drying. (It is safe to use small amounts of foil in newer microwave ovens.) Make several diagonal slashes through the skin of the fish to prevent it from bursting.
- Arrange fillets in a dish with the thicker parts pointing outward and the thinner parts toward center of the dish. Rolled fillets cook more evenly by microwave than flat fillets.
- Cover the dish with plastic wrap and vent by turning back a corner.
- Allow 3 to 6 minutes per pound of boneless fish cooked on high (100% power) as a guide. Rotate the dish halfway through the cooking time.
- Fish may also be poached in a liquid in the microwave. Bring the liquid (fish stock or water and wine) to a boil, then add fish. Cover with plastic wrap and cook as described above.
- Cook side-dishes first and keep them covered while cooking the fish. They will retain heat longer than fish.

## COOKING SHELLFISH IN THE MICROWAVE

- Arrange a single layer of shellfish in a shallow dish and cover with plastic wrap turned back at one corner for venting.
- Allow 2 to 3 minutes per pound of thawed, shucked shellfish cooked on high (100% power). Stir and rotate halfway through the cooking time. Allow to stand for one-third of the cooking time after removing from the oven. (For example, if you cook ½ pound of shucked shellfish for 1 minute and 30 seconds, allow it to stand for 30 seconds before serving.) Be careful not to overcook.
- Place clams, mussels or oysters in the shell in a single layer in a shallow dish. Cover with plastic wrap, venting at one corner. Cook for 2 to 3 minutes on high (100% power). Check and remove pieces as they open. Continue until all have opened. 1 pound will take 12 to 15 minutes.

# TOMATO-BASTED CATFISH STEAKS

- ☐ ¼ cup tomato sauce
- ☐ ¼ cup vinegar
- ☐ ½ tsp. dried dill weed
- ☐ ⅛ tsp. paprika
- ☐ ¼ tsp. pepper

- ☐ ½ tsp. Worcestershire sauce
- ☐ ½ tsp. polyunsaturated vegetable oil
- ☐ 1 lb. catfish fillets or steaks
- ☐ Vegetable cooking spray

## MICROWAVE:
1. Combine tomato sauce with vinegar, spices, Worcestershire sauce and oil in small bowl; stir well.
2. Place catfish in microwave-proof pan. Spread tomato mixture over both sides of fish.
3. Cover and microwave on HIGH 3-6 minutes or until fish just begins to flake. Take out of microwave and let stand a few minutes until fish flakes easily when tested with fork.

## CONVENTIONAL OVEN:
1. Prepare as in 1 above. Then, brush half of mixture over one side of fish. Coat rack of broiler pan with cooking spray. Place steaks on rack; broil 4-5 inches from heat source. Cook 5 minutes.
2. Turn fish over; brush with remaining tomato mixture. Broil an additional 5 minutes or until fish flakes easily when tested with fork. Serve with pasta and fruit plate. **Makes 4 servings.**

*130 calories per serving*
*4.0 grams fat per serving*
*156 mg sodium per serving*
*62 mg cholesterol per serving*

**Substitutions:**
orange roughy, sea bass, flounder

# JAPANESE STYLE COD

*Seafood cooks to moist perfection*
*in the microwave — fast!*

- 1 lb. cod fillets
- 1 T. mayonnaise
- 1 T. light soy sauce
- ½ cup Panko (Japanese-style bread crumbs)
- ⅛ tsp. paprika
- ⅛ tsp. pepper

## MICROWAVE:

1. Place fish in microwave-proof baking dish.
2. Combine mayonnaise, soy sauce, Panko, paprika and pepper in small bowl. Spread mixture over fish.
3. Cover and cook on HIGH for 3-5 minutes, turning dish halfway through cooking time. Remove fish from oven and let sit 3-5 minutes until fish flakes when tested with fork. Serve with steamed rice and vegetables.

## CONVENTIONAL OVEN:

1. Follow directions for microwave method, except place fish in baking pan.
2. Bake in 400° oven until fish flakes when tested with fork. **Makes 4 servings.**

*150 calories per serving*
*4.0 grams fat per serving*
*348 mg sodium per serving*
*46 mg cholesterol per serving*

**Substitutions:**
flounder, Pacific rockfish (snapper), ocean perch

# ZUCCHINI COD AU GRATIN

- ☐ 1 lb. cod fillets
- ☐ Pepper
- ☐ ¼ cup dry white wine
- ☐ 4 cups zucchini, shredded
- ☐ 3 T. Parmesan cheese

- ☐ 6 T. seasoned bread crumbs
- ☐ 2 T. parsley, chopped
- ☐ 2 T. green onion, finely chopped
- ☐ ½ tsp. dried basil

**MICROWAVE:**

1. Cut cod into serving-sized pieces; season with pepper. Sprinkle with wine; let stand 10 minutes. Discard wine after marinating.
2. Combine zucchini, Parmesan cheese, bread crumbs, parsley, green onion and basil in bowl; mix well.
3. Spread half zucchini mixture evenly over bottom of microwave-proof individual serving dishes.
4. Arrange cod on zucchini mixture. Spread remaining zucchini mixture over fish.
5. Microwave covered with waxed paper on HIGH for 3-5 minutes or until fish just flakes when tested with fork. Turn dish halfway through cooking. Remove from oven and let stand for several minutes to complete cooking. **Makes 4 servings.**

*196 calories per serving*
*2.0 grams fat per serving*
*230 mg sodium per serving*
*50 mg cholesterol per serving*

**Substitutions:**
bluefish, haddock, flounder

# FOUR-MINUTE FLOUNDER

*A microwave is a dieter's best friend;*
*it doesn't need added fat and it often intensifies flavors!*

☐ 1 cup water
☐ ½ cup dry white wine
☐ 1 small onion, sliced

☐ 2 sprigs parsley
☐ 5 peppercorns
☐ 1 lb. flounder

## MICROWAVE:

1. In 1-quart microwave-proof bowl combine water, wine, onion, parsley and peppercorns; mix well.
2. Microwave on HIGH 2-3 minutes or until mixture boils.
3. Place flounder in microwave-proof dish; pour wine mixture over flounder.
4. Microwave on HIGH for 3-5 minutes or until fish just begins to flake when tested with fork. Turn dish halfway through cooking time. Remove from oven and let stand to complete cooking. **Makes 4 servings.**

*139 calories per serving*
*1.6 grams fat per serving*
*67 mg sodium per serving*
*56 mg cholesterol per serving*

**Substitutions:**
salmon, cod, black cod

# HERBED HADDOCK

- [ ] 1 lb. haddock
- [ ] 2 T. polyunsaturated margarine
- [ ] 2 T. dry white wine
- [ ] 1 T. green onion, chopped
- [ ] 1 T. parsley, chopped
- [ ] ⅛ tsp. thyme
- [ ] ⅛ tsp. marjoram
- [ ] Lemon slices

## MICROWAVE:

1. Cut fish into serving-sized pieces.
2. Melt margarine in microwave-proof bowl; add remaining ingredients except lemon.
3. Place fish in microwave-proof dish; baste with margarine mixture. Arrange lemon slices on fish.
4. Microwave on HIGH, covered, for 3-5 minutes or until fish just flakes when tested with fork. Turn dish halfway through cooking time, basting fish with margarine mixture. Let stand several minutes to complete cooking. **Makes 4 servings.**

*145 calories per serving*
*6.0 grams fat per serving*
*160 mg sodium per serving*
*68 mg cholesterol per serving*

**Substitutions:**
catfish, pollock, grouper

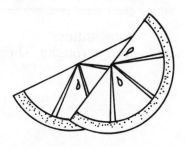

# HOT & SPICY HADDOCK

☐ 1 tsp. onion powder
☐ 2 tsp. curry powder
☐ 1 tsp. cumin
☐ 1 tsp. fresh ginger, grated
  or ½ tsp. ground ginger

☐ ½ tsp. tumeric
☐ ½ clove garlic, minced
☐ 1 lb. haddock

## MICROWAVE:

1. Mix spices together in paper bag. Put fish in bag and shake to coat.
2. Arrange fish in shallow microwave-proof baking dish, placing thickest portions toward outside of dish. Sprinkle with remaining coating. Cover with paper towel.
3. Microwave on HIGH 3-6 minutes, turning dish halfway through cooking time. Microwave just until fish begins to flake when tested with fork. Let stand covered for 2-3 additional minutes.

## CONVENTIONAL OVEN:

1. Mix spices together as in number 1 above.
2. Place fish in baking pan. Sprinkle with remaining coating.
3. Bake, grill or broil fish until it flakes when tested with fork. **Makes 4 servings.**

*80 calories per serving*
*15.0 grams fat per serving*
*60 mg sodium per serving*
*50 mg cholesterol per serving*

**Substitutions:**
croaker, orange roughy, shrimp

# HALIBUT FOR TWO

☐ 1 lb. halibut steaks
  or fillets

☐ 1 T. olive oil

☐ Dash garlic powder

☐ Dash pepper

**MICROWAVE:**

1. Brush fillets or steaks with olive oil. Sprinkle with garlic powder and pepper.

2. Place fish in microwave-proof dish. Cover with paper towel.

3. Microwave on HIGH 3-6 minutes, turning dish halfway through cooking time. Microwave just until fish begins to flake when tested with fork. Let stand covered for 2-3 minutes to continue cooking until fish flakes easily when tested with fork.

**CONVENTIONAL OVEN:**

1. Same as number 1 above.

2. Grill or broil for 8-10 minutes or until fish flakes when tested with fork. Serve with boiled new potatoes and steamed carrots. **Makes 4 servings.**

*150 calories per serving*
*4.9 grams fat per serving*
*68 mg sodium per serving*
*68 mg cholesterol per serving*

**Substitutions:**
Northern pike, lingcod, haddock

# WAIKIKI MAHI MAHI

☐ 1 lb. mahi mahi

☐ Pepper

☐ 1 medium tomato, diced

☐ ¼ cup fresh
   mushrooms, sliced

☐ ¼ cup onion, sliced

☐ ¼ cup celery, diced

☐ 1 T. lemon juice

☐ 1 T. polyunsaturated oil

☐ ¼ tsp. thyme

☐ Dash pepper

☐ Chopped parsley

## MICROWAVE:

1. Sprinkle mahi mahi with pepper and place in microwave-proof dish. Spoon tomato over fish.

2. In microwave-proof bowl combine mushrooms, onion, celery, lemon juice, oil, thyme, and dash of pepper; mix well. Microwave on HIGH, covered with plastic wrap for 2-3 minutes or until tender-crisp.

3. Spoon vegetable mixture over fish. Microwave on HIGH, covered, for 3-5 minutes or until fish just flakes when tested with fork. Let stand several minutes to complete cooking. Garnish with parlsey. **Makes 4 servings.**

*162 calories per serving*
*4.7 grams fat per serving*
*160 mg sodium per serving*
*96 mg cholesterol per serving*

**Substitutions:**
grouper, tilefish, trout

# HERB-CRUMBED ORANGE ROUGHY

☐ 1 lb. orange roughy

☐ 1 T. olive oil

☐ ¼ cup seasoned
   bread crumbs

☐ 1 T. parsley,
   finely chopped

☐ Pepper to taste

☐ ⅛ tsp. dried thyme,
   crushed

**MICROWAVE:**

1. Place fish in microwave-proof dish. Brush with olive oil. Combine bread crumbs, parsley, pepper and thyme. Sprinkle the seasoned crumb mixture onto the fish. Cover with paper towel.

2. Microwave for 3-6 minutes per pound, turning dish halfway through cooking time. Microwave until fish just begins to flake when tested with fork.

3. Let stand covered for additional 2-3 minutes or until fish flakes when tested with fork.

**CONVENTIONAL OVEN:**

1. Place fish in baking pan. Brush with olive oil. Combine bread crumbs, parlsey, pepper and thyme. Sprinkle the seasoned crumb mixture onto the fish.

2. Bake in 450⁰ oven for about 10 minutes or until fish flakes when tested with fork. Serve immediately with wedges of lemon or lime. **Makes 4 servings.**

*125 calories per serving*
*4.0 grams fat per serving*
*110 mg sodium per serving*
*22 mg cholesterol per serving*

**Substitutions:**
Pacific rockfish (snapper), cod

# CAJUN BAKED ROCKFISH (SNAPPER)

☐ ⅓ cup light mayonnaise
☐ ½ tsp. ground cumin
☐ ½ tsp. onion powder
☐ ¼ tsp. ground red pepper

☐ ¼ tsp. garlic powder
☐ 1 lb. Pacific rockfish (snapper) fillets
☐ 8 sesame crackers, crushed

## MICROWAVE:

1. Combine mayonnaise and seasonings in bowl. Brush red snapper with mayonnaise mixture; coat with sesame cracker crumbs.

2. Arrange fish in shallow microwave-proof baking dish, placing thickest portions toward outside of dish. Cover with paper towel. Microwave on HIGH 3-6 minutes; turning dish halfway through cooking time until fish just begins to flake when tested with fork. Let stand, covered, 2-3 minutes to complete cooking.

## CONVENTIONAL OVEN:

1. Combine mayonnaise and seasoning in bowl.

2. Brush red snapper with mayonnaise mixture; coat with sesame cracker crumbs.

3. Place in baking dish. Bake in 400° oven for 15-20 minutes or until fish flakes when tested with fork. Serve with corn meal muffins and steamed vegetables. **Makes 4 servings.**

*168 calories per serving*
*6.8 grams fat per serving*
*177 mg sodium per serving*
*45 mg cholesterol per serving*

**Substitutions:**
catfish, tilefish

# POPEYE'S SALMON

- ☐ 1 lb. salmon fillets, skinless and boneless
- ☐ Pepper to taste
- ☐ 1 medium onion, thinly sliced and halved
- ☐ 1 T. polyunsaturated margarine

- ☐ 4 cups packed spinach leaves (about 8 oz.) or 8 oz. frozen whole spinach, thawed and drained
- ☐ 1 tsp. lemon juice
- ☐ 1 tsp. olive oil
- ☐ ½ tsp. light soy sauce
- ☐ ¼ tsp. sugar

**MICROWAVE:**

1. Season salmon with pepper; place in microwave-proof dish. Microwave covered with plastic wrap at HIGH power 3-5 minutes or until fish just flakes when tested with fork. Turn dish halfway through cooking time. Keep warm.

2. Place onion and margarine on large microwave-proof serving platter. Microwave covered with plastic wrap at HIGH 3 minutes or until onion is tender: turn dish halfway through cooking.

3. Place spinach leaves over onion mixture. Microwave, covered, on HIGH 2 minutes or until spinach is wilted.

4. Combine lemon juice, olive oil, soy sauce and sugar; mix well. Drizzle over spinach. Place salmon on spinach mixture. **Makes 4 servings.**

*221 calories per serving*
*11.0 grams fat per serving*
*192 mg sodium per serving*
*73 mg cholesterol per serving*

**Substitutions:**
ocean perch, orange roughy, bluefish

# GINGER-SESAME SOLE FILLETS

- ☐ ½ T. sesame seeds
- ☐ 2 tsp. fresh ginger, minced
- ☐ 1 clove garlic, minced
- ☐ 1 T. sesame oil
- ☐ 1 tsp. light soy sauce
- ☐ 1 lb. sole fillets
- ☐ Pepper to taste
- ☐ 1 T. fresh ginger, thinly slivered

## MICROWAVE:

1. Toast sesame seeds in small dry skillet over low heat.
2. Combine minced ginger and garlic, sesame oil and soy sauce in small bowl; set aside.
3. Season fillets lightly with pepper and arrange in single layer in microwave-proof baking dish.
4. Spread ginger mixture over fillets, then sprinkle with slivered ginger.
5. Cover dish with plastic wrap. Microwave on HIGH for 3-5 minutes, turning dish halfway through cooking time. Remove from oven and let stand until fish flakes when tested with fork.
6. Sprinkle with sesame seeds and serve. **Makes 4 servings.**

*140 calories per serving*
*4.7 grams fat per serving*
*260 mg sodium per serving*
*50 mg cholesterol per serving*

**Substitutions:**
grouper, flounder, tilefish, trout

# HOLIDAY SEAFOOD WITH CHAMPAGNE

*Microwave in minutes*

- ☐ 2 lbs. firm fish fillets, boneless and skinless
- ☐ 1 cup champagne
- ☐ 1 cup mushrooms, sliced
- ☐ 1 cup onions, sliced thin in rings
- ☐ 1 T. polyunsaturated margarine
- ☐ 1 cup plain low fat yogurt
- ☐ 1 T. cornstarch
- ☐ 1 cup part-skim Mozzarella cheese, grated
- ☐ 1 tsp. dried tarragon
- ☐ ½ tsp. white pepper
- ☐ Paprika

**MICROWAVE:**

1. Place fish fillets in microwave-proof pan. Cover with champagne and marinate for 10 minutes.
2. Microwave mushrooms and onions in margarine for 4 minutes in separate microwave-proof container.
3. Drain champagne from fish. Discard.
4. Mix yogurt, cornstarch, Mozzarella cheese, tarragon and white pepper together. Spread over fish. Spread vegetables over fish and top with paprika.
5. Cover and microwave on HIGH for 5-10 minutes or until fish just begins to flake when tested with fork. Turn dish halfway through cooking time. Let stand for several minutes to complete cooking. **Makes 8 servings.**

*223 calories per serving*
*7.3 grams fat per serving*
*225 mg sodium per serving*
*87 mg cholesterol per serving*

**Substitutions:**
halibut, Pacific rockfish (snapper), cod

# OYSTERS PARMESAN

*Oysters are an excellent source of iron and are low in cholesterol and calories.*

- ☐ ¼ cup green onion, chopped
- ☐ ¼ cup fresh parsley, chopped
- ☐ 3 cloves garlic, minced
- ☐ 2 tsp. polyunsaturated margarine
- ☐ 1 T. lime juice
- ☐ 4 drops hot pepper sauce (Tabasco)
- ☐ 1 jar (10 oz.) small oysters
- ☐ ¼ tsp. cracked black pepper
- ☐ ¼ cup Parmesan cheese
- ☐ ¼ cup bread crumbs

## MICROWAVE:
1. Place green onion, parsley, garlic, margarine, lime juice and Tabasco in microwave-proof dish. Stir; microwave on HIGH for 1 minute.
2. Add oysters to dish and stir to coat with mixture. Sprinkle pepper, Parmesan cheese and bread crumbs over top of oysters.
3. Microwave on HIGH for 3-5 minutes or until oysters are done. Can be served in individual seafood shells as an appetizer or as an entree. **Makes 2-4 servings.**

*130 calories per serving*
*4.5 grams fat per serving*
*23 mg sodium per serving*
*39 mg cholesterol per serving*

**Substitutions:**
mussels

# CANCUN SHRIMP

- ☐ 2 T. olive oil
- ☐ 2 cloves garlic, minced
- ☐ 2 lbs. shrimp or prawns, peeled and deveined
- ☐ Cumin
- ☐ Lemon juice
- ☐ Pepper to taste

**MICROWAVE:**

1. Microwave olive oil with garlic on HIGH for 30 seconds in microwave-proof dish.
2. Stir in shrimp with cumin, lemon juice and pepper. Arrange shrimp/prawns in single layer.
3. Cover casserole tightly and cook on HIGH for 2-3 minutes, stirring every minute until shrimp just begin to turn opaque. Remove from oven and let stand additional 2-3 minutes to complete cooking. Serve hot or cold with bowl of cocktail sauce on side. Can also be prepared and served with shells. **Makes 8 servings or several appetizers.**

*132 calories per serving*
*4.4 grams fat per serving*
*158 mg sodium per serving*
*178 mg cholesterol per serving*

**Substitutions:**
oysters, crayfish, lobster

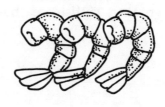

# GARLIC SHRIMP

- [ ] 6 cloves garlic, coarsely chopped
- [ ] 2 T. olive oil
- [ ] 1 tsp. red chile pepper, seeded and minced or ½ tsp. dried red pepper flakes

- [ ] 2 lbs. large shrimp or prawns, peeled and deveined
- [ ] 1 T. lime juice

## MICROWAVE:
1. Microwave garlic in oil on HIGH for 1 minute.
2. Add chile pepper and shrimp and cover; microwave on HIGH for 1 minute.
3. Add lime juice and cook an additional 2 minutes or until shrimp begin to turn opaque. Let stand 2-3 additional minutes to complete cooking.

## CONVENTIONAL OVEN:
1. Saute garlic in oil in large, heavy skillet over medium-high heat for 1 minute.
2. Add chile pepper and shrimp and cook 4 minutes, stirring constantly.
3. Add lime juice and cook an additional 2 minutes or until shrimp turn opaque. Serve as an appetizer or entree. **Makes 8 servings.**

*133 calories per serving*
*4.4 grams fat per serving*
*158 mg sodium per serving*
*178 mg cholesterol per serving*

**Substitutions:**
croaker, catfish, sea bass

# SAUCES

## CHAPTER 8
# SAUCES

# BASIC PREPARATION METHODS

The following preparation methods serve as basic guidelines to preparing seafood in a heart-healthy manner.

1. Select a sauce from this chapter.
2. Select desired seafood.
3. Prepare and serve seafood and sauce as per recipe directions.

• **BAKE**
Place seafood in baking dish. Add sauce or topping to keep moist. Cover and bake at 400-450ºF. until done.

• **BROIL**
Place seafood in broiler pan. Brush with marinade, sauce, a small amount of polyunsaturate margarine or other topping. Flavor as desired. Broil 4-5 inches from heat source without turning. Cook until done.

• **POACH**
Estimate amount of liquid needed to cover seafood in poaching pan or saucepan. Liquids could include skim milk, water, low-salt chicken broth or wine. Season as desired. Bring to boil; cover & simmer about 10 minutes. Add seafood and bring to boil. Reduce heat and simmer until done.

• **STEAMING**
Place seafood on a steaming rack, set 2 inches above boiling liquid, in deep pot. Season as desired. Cover tightly. Reduce heat and steam until done.

• **GRILLING OR BARBECUING**
Place seafood on lightly-oiled grill. Baste with sauce or marinade as desired. Turn halfway through cooking time. Continue to baste throughout cooking time. Cook until done.

• **SAUTEING**
Heat a small amount of polyunsaturated margarine or oil with
liquid, such as white wine,
in frying pan or saute pan.
Add vegetables as desired.
Add seafood and saute over
medium heat until done.

• **MICROWAVE**
See pages 105, 106.

# CORN AND TOMATO SALSA

*One of our favorites*

♥ *Excellent as a sauce on a seafood tostada.*

- ☐ ½ cup onion, finely chopped
- ☐ 1 large, ripe tomato, chopped
- ☐ 1 box frozen corn
- ☐ Juice from 1 lime
- ☐ 1 tsp. ground cumin
- ☐ 1 tsp. garlic powder
- ☐ 1 can (4 oz.) green chiles, chopped

1. Mix all ingredients together in medium-size bowl. Let stand until frozen corn is thawed. Serve chilled on barbecued seafood or cold poached fish. **Makes 4 servings. Sauce for 1 lb. of seafood.**

*47 calories per serving*
*0.7 gram fat per serving*
*30 mg sodium per serving*
*0 mg cholesterol per serving*

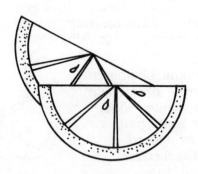

# TERIYAKI MARINADE

- ☐ 1½ T. pineapple juice
- ☐ 1½ T. light soy sauce
- ☐ 1 T. polyunsaturated oil
- ☐ 1 T. sherry

- ☐ 1 T. fresh ginger, grated
- ☐ ¼ tsp. dry mustard
- ☐ 1 clove garlic, minced
- ☐ ½ tsp. brown sugar

1. Combine ingredients in bowl.
2. Pour marinade over fish and marinate about 15 minutes, turning over once.
3. Drain fish, reserving marinade.
4. Prepare fish for cooking. Baste with marinade as fish cooks. Suggested methods of cooking include grilling, broiling, steaming, or microwaving. Marinade may be reserved in the refrigerator for up to 2 weeks. **Makes 4 servings. Marinade for 1 lb. of seafood.**

*40 calories per serving*
*3.6 grams fat per serving*
*246 mg sodium per serving*
*0 mg cholesterol per serving*

# ORIENTAL MARINADE

□ 2 T. orange juice

□ 2 T. light soy sauce

□ 1 T. catsup

□ 1 T. polyunsaturated oil

□ 1 T. parsley, chopped

□ 1 T. lemon juice

□ ½ clove garlic, minced

□ Dash pepper

1. Combine all marinade ingredients in bowl. Pour marinade over fish and let stand for 15 minutes, turning once.

2. Drain fish, reserving marinade. Grill, broil or steam fish as desired, basting with sauce during cooking. **Makes 8 servings. Marinade for 2 lbs. of seafood.**

*22 calories per serving*
*1.8 grams fat per serving*
*215 mg sodium per serving*
*0 mg cholesterol per serving*

# TARRAGON MUSTARD SAUCE

☐ 2 T. tarragon vinegar
☐ 2 T. Dijon mustard
☐ 1 tsp. dried tarragon

☐ ¼ cup plus 2 T. plain low fat yogurt
☐ ¼ cup light mayonnaise

1. Combine tarragon vinegar, mustard and dried tarragon in small bowl.
2. Add yogurt and mayonnaise; stir until well blended. Spread over fish. Bake or microwave seafood.
3. Alternative method: serve over cooked seafood such as leftover grilled or cold poached seafood. **Makes 6 servings. Sauce for 1½ lbs. seafood.**

*45 calories per serving*
*4.0 grams fat per serving*
*142 mg sodium per serving*
*0 mg cholesterol per serving*

# SWEET AND SOUR SAUCE
*Family favorite*

- ☐ 1 small onion, chopped
- ☐ ¼ cup catsup
- ☐ 1 jar (2 oz.) pimiento, sliced
- ☐ 1 T. polyunsaturated oil
- ☐ ¼ cup white wine vinegar
- ☐ 1 T. Worcestershire sauce
- ☐ ½ tsp. pepper
- ☐ 1 tsp. paprika

- ☐ 2 tsp. chili powder
- ☐ 1 tsp. fresh garlic, minced
- ☐ 1 tsp. fresh ginger, minced
- ☐ 2 T. sugar
- ☐ 1 cup water
- ☐ 1 cup mushrooms, sliced

1. Combine all ingredients in saucepan.
2. Bring to boil; lower heat and simmer at least fifteen minutes; set aside.
3. Pour sauce over seafood and bake or broil as desired; or pour heated sauce over grilled seafood. Sauce may be refrigerated for 2 weeks. **Makes 6 servings. Sauce for 1½ lbs. of seafood.**

*46 calories per serving*
*0 grams fat per serving*
*130 mg sodium per serving*
*0 mg cholesterol per serving*

# WINE SAUCE
### Excellent as a saute sauce

- ☐ 1 T. olive oil
- ☐ 3 T. dry white wine
- ☐ 2 T. parsley, minced
- ☐ 2 cloves garlic, minced
- ☐ Pepper

1. Combine all ingredients in bowl. Brush on fish and broil or grill seafood as desired. **Makes 4 servings. Sauce for 1 lb. of seafood.**

*44 calories per serving*
*3.5 grams fat per serving*
*0 mg sodium per serving*
*0 mg cholesterol per serving*

# LIGHT & SPICY SAUCE

☐ 1 T. polyunsaturated oil     ☐ ½ tsp. garlic, minced
☐ 1 T. parsley, finely chopped     ☐ ¼ tsp. pepper
☐ 1 T. light soy sauce     ☐ 3 T. lemon juice
☐ 1 tsp. Worcestershire sauce

1. In small mixing bowl combine all ingredients. Marinate fish briefly before cooking; brush on marinade during baking, microwaving, or broiling. **Makes 4 servings. Sauce for 1 lb. of seafood.**

*41 calories per serving*
*3.5 grams fat per serving*
*210 mg sodium per serving*
*0 mg cholesterol per serving*

# RED PEPPER SAUCE

- ☐ 1 T. olive oil
- ☐ 1 T. shallots, chopped
- ☐ 3 cloves garlic, chopped
- ☐ 1 T. parsley, chopped

- ☐ 1 medium red pepper, sliced into narrow strips
- ☐ ⅛ tsp. cayenne pepper
- ☐ ¼ tsp. pepper

1. In small saute pan, heat olive oil; add shallots and garlic. Saute until tender.
2. Add parsley, red peppers, cayenne and pepper; saute until pepper is tender-crisp. Remove from heat. Set aside. Makes excellent topping for grilled fish. **Makes 4 servings. Sauce for 1 lb. of seafood.**

*37 calories per serving*
*3.5 grams fat per serving*
*6.5 mg sodium per serving*
*0 mg cholesterol per serving*

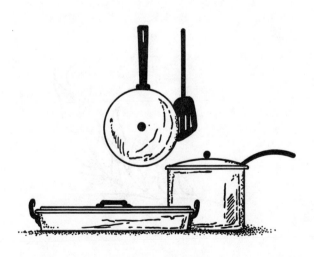

# MEXICALI SAUCE

- ☐ 1¼ cups prepared chunky salsa
- ☐ 1 T. lime juice
- ☐ ½ tsp. dried oregano
- ☐ ½ clove garlic, minced
- ☐ ¼ tsp. cumin
- ☐ Fresh lime wedges

1. Combine salsa, lime juice, oregano, garlic and cumin in small bowl; set aside.
2. Spread sauce over prepared fish (baking, steaming or poaching are good methods) and serve with lime wedges. Makes 4 servings. Sauce for 1 lb. of seafood.

*20 calories per serving*
*0 grams fat per serving*
*100 mg sodium per serving*
*0 mg cholesterol per serving*

LIGHT-HEARTED SEAFOOD

# LEMON-GARLIC SAUCE

*Excellent as a saute sauce.*

♥ *Save time by peeling garlic in advance and storing it, covered with olive oil, in a jar. It will stay fresh for at least two weeks in the refrigerator and perk up the oil, too.*

☐ 1 T. polyunsaturated margarine, melted

☐ 1 clove garlic, finely chopped

☐ 2 T. lemon juice

☐ Pinch pepper

☐ Fresh parsley, chopped

1. In small saucepan, melt margarine. Add garlic and saute until tender. Remove from heat. Add lemon juice, pepper and parsley. Spread over fish and cook as desired.

## MICROWAVE:

1. Microwave margarine and garlic on HIGH until tender (about 1 minute) in microwave-proof pan. Add lemon juice, pepper and parsley. Spread over fish and cook as desired. **Makes 4 servings. Sauce for 1 lb. of seafood.**

*25 calories per serving*
*3.0 grams fat per serving*
*35 mg sodium per serving*
*0 mg cholesterol per serving*

# SCAMPI SAUCE

- ☐ 1 tsp. olive oil
- ☐ 4 cloves garlic, minced
- ☐ 2 T. dry vermouth
- ☐ 1 tsp. dried red pepper flakes
- ☐ 1 tsp. paprika
- ☐ 1 T. lemon juice
- ☐ ½ cup fresh parsley, chopped

1. Heat oil in saute pan; add garlic and cook over medium heat until tender.
2. Stir in vermouth, pepper flakes, paprika and lemon juice. Brush on fish and cook in desired manner.

**MICROWAVE:**

1. Combine oil and garlic in 10-inch pie plate. Cook on HIGH for 1-2 minutes or until tender.
2. Stir in vermouth, pepper flakes, paprika and lemon juice. Brush on fish and bake or grill. **Makes 4 servings. Sauce for 1 lb. of seafood.**

*15 calories per serving*
*1.2 grams fat per serving*
*0 mg sodium per serving*
*0 mg cholesterol per serving*

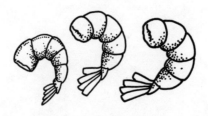

# ITALIAN-STYLE SAUCE

- ☐ 1 T. olive oil
- ☐ Juice from 1 lemon (about 2 T.)
- ☐ ¼ tsp. garlic powder
- ☐ ¼ tsp. onion powder
- ☐ 1 T. Italian Seafood Seasoning (see page 138)

1. In large bowl, mix olive oil, lemon juice, garlic, onion powder and Italian Seafood Seasoning.
2. Add seafood into seasoning bowl and coat thoroughly.
3. Saute, bake or grill seafood as desired. **Makes 4 servings. Sauce for 1 lb. of seafood.**

*38 calories per serving*
*3.5 grams fat per serving*
*0 mg sodium per serving*
*0 mg cholesterol per serving*

# ITALIAN
# SEAFOOD SEASONING

*Great all around spice mixture for seafood preparation.*

☐ 2 tsp. dried rosemary      ☐ 2 T. dried thyme
☐ 2 T. dried oregano        ☐ 3 T. dried basil
☐ 3 T. dried marjoram

1. Mix all ingredients together. Grind in blender or food processor until finely ground.
2. Place in jar and cover tightly.
3. Shake before using. Shake on microwave, baked or grilled seafood.

*0 calories per serving*
*0 grams fat per serving*
*0 mg sodium per serving*
*0 mg cholesterol per serving*

# GENERAL

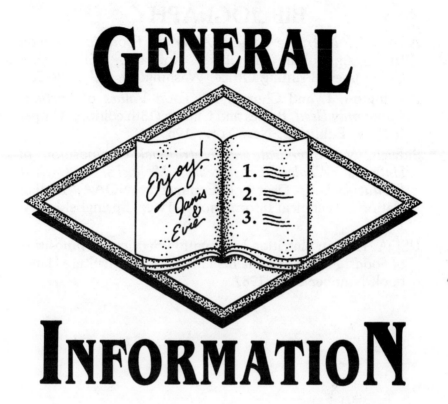

Enjoy!
Janis
&
Evie

1.
2.
3.

# INFORMATION

# BIBLIOGRAPHY

Adams, C.: *Nutritive Value of American Foods in Common Units*, Agriculture Handbook No. 456, USDA, U.S. Government Printing Office, Washington, D.C., 1975.

Pennington, J. and Church, H.: *Food Values of Portions Commonly Used*, Bowes and Church (13th edition). Harper & Row, Publisher, New York, 1980.

Sidwell, V.: *Chemical and Nutritional Composition of Finfishes, Whales, Crustaceans, Mollusks, and Their Products*, U.S. Dept. of Commerce, NOAA, NMFS, National Technical Information Service, Springfield, VA, 1985.

USDA, Human Nutrition Information Service: *Composition of Foods: Finfish and Shellfish Products*, Agriculture Handbook Number 8-15, 1987.

# ABOUT THE AUTHORS

Practically born into the world of seafood, both Janis Harsila and Evie Hansen were reared in families who relied on the commercial fishing industry for their earnings. Later, both married commercial fishermen. They met on a fishing dock in the San Juan Islands in the state of Washington. A fast friendship grew into a solid partnership when they both realized they shared a deep love of seafood. Moreover, each had a commitment to bring their world to those who want to eat fish but know little of how to handle, prepare or serve it. National Seafood Educators was formed in 1977 to provide education, training and recipe development to retailers, health professionals and consumers and to make the culinary pleasures of healthful seafood accessible to all.

In 1983, National Seafood Educators introduced one of the first seafood and health awareness programs in the nation. Their efforts were recognized by the American Heart Association — Washington Affiliate who as co-sponsors, produced a seafood consumer awareness campaign called, "Seafood Is Heart Food", which was used throughout the nation. In 1986, National Seafood Educators published a highly-regarded, seafood cookbook called *Seafood: A Collection of Heart-Healthy Recipes.* The book, now in its fifth printing, is recommended by the American Dietetic Association, the Tufts University Diet and Nutrition Letter and the Center for Science in the Public Interest. Additionally, it has been endorsed by the *Los Angeles Times, Washington Post, Seattle Times, Dallas Morning News*, the *Oregonian*, the *Boston Globe, Parade, Cosmopolitan, Cooking Light* and a host of other consumer publications.

**Janis Harsila,** Director of Nutrition Education, is a registered dietitian. She keeps up-to-date on the latest research linking seafood diets with health benefits. She also educates health care professionals and consumers in the links between seafood and health. Harsila knows how to prepare flavorful meals which can keep people both happy and healthy. She is a member of the American Dietetic Association and Omicron Nu Honor Society.

**Evie Hansen,** Director of Seafood Marketing, has a lifetime of experience in consulting. Formerly a special education teacher, Hansen utilizes her training with retailers, offering them needed skills in seafood marketing and merchandising. Hansen completed a seafood merchandising program at Oregon State University and was the recipient of a Seafood Quality Control Certificate from the University of Washington. In addition, she is the co-author of a merchandising manual, *Selling Seafood,* published by the Alaska Seafood Marketing Institute, which has been sold in over twelve countries. She has been selected to appear in *Who's Who in Business and Finance* and *Who's Who in the West in 1989.*

# ORDERING INFORMATION

*For more copies of* **Light-Hearted Seafood:**

|  | | Quantity Purchases | |
|---|---|---|---|
| Price per book | $10.95 | 3 books | $29.95 |
| Tax for WA state residents | $ .89 | Tax for WA state residents | $ 2.43 |
| Postage and Handling | $2.00 | Postage and Handling | $ 4.00 |

*For copies of our first cookbook,* **Seafood: A Collection of Heart-Healthy Recipes:**

|  | | Quantity Purchases | |
|---|---|---|---|
| Price per book | $11.95 | 3 books | $32.95 |
| Tax for WA state residents | $ .97 | Tax for WA state residents | $ 2.67 |
| Postage and Handling | $ 2.00 | Postage and Handling | $ 4.00 |

Send personal check, VISA or MASTERCARD number (with expiration date) to:

**National Seafood Educators**
P.O. Box 60006
Richmond Beach, WA 98160
(206) 546-6410

# DIABETIC EXCHANGES

| RECIPE | Pg. No. | Bread | MEAT lean | MEAT med. | MEAT high | Veg. | Fruit | MILK skim | MILK low | MILK whole | Fat | COMMENTS |
|---|---|---|---|---|---|---|---|---|---|---|---|---|
| Salmon Cheesecake | 29 | 1 | | | | | | | ½ | | ½ | |
| Lomi Lomi Salmon | 30 | 1 | | | | 1 | | | | | | |
| Creamy Clam Dip | 31 | ½ | | | | | | | | | | |
| Flintstone Seafood Dip | 32 | ¼ | | | | ¼ | | | | | | |
| Light & Versatile Dill Dressing | 33 | | | | | | | | | | ½ | |
| Aleck Bay Steamer Clams | 34 | 2 | 2 | | | | 1 | | | | | Fruit for alcohol calories |
| Mussels on the Half Shell | 35 | ½ | 1½ | | | | | | | | | |
| Herb Stuffed Oysters | 36 | 1 | | | | ½ | | | | | | |
| Bay Scallops & Shrimp in Pasta Shells | 37 | 2 | 2 | | | 1 | | | | | | |
| Shrimp & Cucumber Salad | 38 | 1 | | | | 1 | | | | | | |
| Marinated Halibut Salad | 41 | 3½ | | | | 1 | 1 | | | | | Allow 1 fat ex. extra |
| Tarragon Salmon Salad | 42 | 1½ | | | | 1 | | | | | | |
| Sweet & Sour Tuna Salad | 43 | 2 | | | | 1½ | 1½ | | | | | |
| Greek Style Salad | 44 | 2½ | | | | 2 | | | | | | |
| Seashell Salad | 45 | 2 | 1½ | | | 2 | | | | | | |
| Chinese Seafood Salad | 46 | 1 | 1 | | | 3 | | | | | ½ | |
| Pasta & Crab Salad | 47 | 1 | ½ | | | 1 | | | | | | |
| Sensational Seafood Salad | 48 | 1 | | | | 2 | | | | | | |
| Cilantro Potato Salad | 49 | 2 | ½ | | | 1 | | | | | | |
| Marinated Spanish Seafood Salad | 50 | 2½ | | | | 2 | | | | | | Allow 1 fat ex. extra |

| RECIPE | Pg. No. | Bread | MEAT lean | MEAT med. | MEAT high | Veg. | Fruit | MILK skim | MILK low | MILK whole | Fat | COMMENTS |
|---|---|---|---|---|---|---|---|---|---|---|---|---|
| Curry Shrimp & Rice Salad | 51 | 1 | 1 | | | 1 | | | | | | |
| Shrimp Coleslaw | 52 | | 1 | | | 1 | | | | | | Allow ½ fat ex. extra |
| Lunchbox Tuna or Salmon Sandwich | 57 | 2 | 2 | | | 3 | | | | | | Allow ½ fat ex. extra salmon sandwich |
| Tuna Melt Supreme | 58 | 1 | 2 | | | ½ | | | | | | Allow ½ fat ex. extra |
| Open-faced Crab Muffin | 59 | 1 | ½ | | | | ½ | | | | | |
| Shrimp Topped Rice Cakes | 60 | ½ | | ½ | | | | | | | | |
| Highliner's Choice Salmon Chowder | 61 | 1 | 2 | 1 | | ½ | | | | | | |
| Manhattan Shellfish Chowder | 62 | | 2 | | | 2 | 1 | | | | | Fruit for alcohol calories |
| Norwegian Crab Bisque | 63 | 1 | 2 | | | 4 | | 1 | | | | Allow 1 fat ex. extra |
| Bourbon Street Gumbo | 64 | ½ | 3 | | | 1 | | | | | | |
| Corn & Tomato Salsa | 126 | ½ | | | | 1 | | | | | | |
| Teriyaki Marinade | 127 | | | | | ½ | | | | | ¾ | |
| Oriental Marinade | 128 | | | | | ½ | | | | | ⅓ | |
| Tarragon Mustard Sauce | 129 | | | | | ½ | | | | | ¾ | |
| Sweet & Sour Sauce | 130 | | | | | 1 | ½ | | | | | |
| Wine Sauce | 131 | | | | | ¼ | | | | | ¾ | |
| Light & Spicy Sauce | 132 | | | | | ½ | | | | | ¾ | |
| Red Pepper Sauce | 133 | | | | | ½ | | | | | ¾ | |
| Mexicali Sauce | 134 | | | | | 1 | | | | | | |
| Lemon-Garlic Sauce | 135 | | | | | | ⅓ | | | | ¾ | |
| Scampi Sauce | 136 | | | | | 1 | | | | | | |
| Italian-Style Sauce | 137 | | | | | ½ | | | | | ¾ | |

| RECIPE | Pg. No. | Bread | MEAT | | | Veg. | Fruit | MILK | | | Fat | COMMENTS |
|---|---|---|---|---|---|---|---|---|---|---|---|---|
| | | | lean | med. | high | | | skim | low | whole | | |
| Italian Seafood Seasoning | 138 | | | | | | | | | | | Free Food |
| Bluefish Dijon | 69 | | 3 | | | ¼ | | | | | | Allow ½ fat ex. extra |
| Ocean Cod Supreme | 70 | | 2½ | | | | | ½ | ⅓ | | | Allow 1 fat ex. extra. Fruit for alcohol. |
| Country Garden Saute | 71 | | 3 | | | 3 | | | | | | Allow 1 fat ex. extra |
| Cucumber Haddock | 72 | | 3 | | | 2 | | | | | | Allow 1½ fat ex. extra |
| Casserole Delight | 73 | | 4 | | | 1 | 1 | | | | | Fruit for alcohol calories |
| Best Dressed Mackerel | 74 | | 2 | | | | | | | | 1 | |
| Best Dressed Trout | 74 | | | 2 | | | | | | | 1 | |
| Monkfish Saute | 75 | | 2 | | | 1½ | | | | | | |
| Orange Roughy with Tomato-Tarragon Sauce | 76 | | 2 | | | 2 | | | | | | Allow ½ fat ex. extra |
| Cheesey Rockfish | 77 | ½ | 3 | | | | | | | | | Allow ½ fat ex. extra |
| Poached Sablefish | 78 | | 3 | | | ½ | | | | | | Allow ½ fat ex. extra |
| Bristol Bay Salmon | 79 | | 3 | | | | | | | | | |
| Thai-style Salmon Potato | 80 | 1 | 3 | 1 | | 3 | | | | | | |
| Curried Salmon | 81 | | 3 | | | 1 | 1 | | | | | ½ fruit ex. for fruit, ½ fruit ex. for alcohol. |
| Savory Salmon Loaf | 82 | ½ | 2½ | | | | | | | | | |
| Slender Steamed Sole | 83 | | 2½ | | | | | | | | | Allow 1 fat ex. extra |
| Heartfelt Sole | 84 | | 2½ | | | | ½ | | | | | Allow ½ fat ex. extra. Fruit for alcohol. |
| Columbia River Sturgeon | 85 | | 2 | | | | | | | | ½ | |
| Swordfish & Herbs | 86 | | 3 | | | 1 | 1 | | | | | Fruit for wine calories |
| Szechwan Stirfry | 87 | | 2 | | | 2 | | | | | | |
| Savory Tuna for Four | 88 | | 2½ | | | 4 | | ½ | | | | Allow ½ fat ex. extra |

146

| RECIPE | Pg. No. | Bread | MEAT lean | MEAT med. | MEAT high | Veg. | Fruit | MILK skim | MILK low | MILK whole | Fat | COMMENTS |
|---|---|---|---|---|---|---|---|---|---|---|---|---|
| Mother's Oyster Pie | 92 | 2 | 1 | | | | | | | | ½ | |
| Romantic Scallops For Two | 93 | | 1½ | | | 1 | | | | | | |
| Prawn and Scallop Saute | 94 | | 3 | | | 1 | | | | | | |
| Spicy Poached Shrimp | 95 | | 3 | | | | | | | | | Allow 2 fat ex. extra |
| Italian Fisherman's Spaghetti | 96 | | 1 | | | 1½ | | | | | | |
| Shrimp & Tomato Tostada | 97 | 1 | 1 | | | 3 | | | | | | |
| Phillipine Pansit | 98 | 1 | 1 | | | 2 | | | | | | |
| Spinach Fettucine With Shrimp | 99 | 1 | 1½ | | | 3 | ½ | | | | ½ | |
| Saucy Squid | 100 | ½ | 2 | | | 2 | | | | | | |
| Stuffed Squid Supreme | 101 | | 1 | 1 | | 2 | 1 | | | | | |
| Tomato-Basted Catfish Steaks | 107 | | 3 | | | ½ | | | | | | Allow 1 fat ex. extra |
| Japanese-Style Cod | 108 | ½ | 2½ | | | | | | | | | Allow ½ fat ex. extra |
| Zucchini Cod Au Gratin | 109 | 1 | 2½ | | | 3 | | | | | | Allow 1 fat ex. extra |
| Four-Minute Flounder | 110 | | 3 | | | ½ | ½ | | | | | Allow 1½ fat ex. extra. Fruit for alcohol. |
| Herbed Haddock | 111 | | 3 | | | ½ | | | | | | Allow ½ fat ex. extra |
| Hot & Spicy Haddock | 112 | | 3 | | | | | | | | | Allow 1½ fat ex. extra |
| Halibut For Two | 113 | | 3½ | | | | | | | | | Allow 1 fat ex. extra |
| Waikiki Mahi Mahi | 114 | | 3 | | | 1 | | | | | | Allow 1 fat ex. extra |
| Herb-Crumbed Orange Roughy | 115 | | 2½ | | | | | | | | | Allow ½ fat ex. extra |
| Cajun Baked Rockfish | 116 | ⅓ | 3 | | | | | | | | | Allow ½ fat ex. extra |
| Popeye's Salmon | 117 | | 3½ | | | 1 | | | | | | |
| Ginger-Sesame Sole Fillets | 118 | | 2½ | | | | | | | | | Allow ½ fat ex. extra |

| RECIPE | Pg. No. | Bread | MEAT | | | Veg. | Fruit | MILK | | | Fat | COMMENTS |
|---|---|---|---|---|---|---|---|---|---|---|---|---|
| | | | lean | med. | high | | | skim | low | whole | | |
| Holiday Seafood With Champagne | 119 | | 4 | | | 1 | | | | | | Allow 1 fat ex. extra |
| Oysters Parmesan | 120 | ½ | 1½ | | | 1 | | | | | | |
| Cancun Shrimp | 121 | | 3 | | | | | | | | | Allow 1 fat ex. extra |
| Garlic Shrimp | 122 | | 3 | | | | | | | | | Allow 1 fat ex. extra |

ex. - exchange

# INDEX BY TITLE

# INDEX

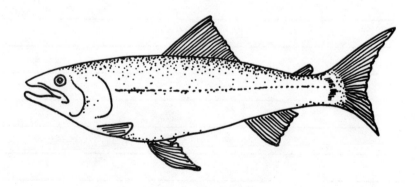

*We would love to hear from you...send us your favorite recipes and ideas!*

_____

_____

_____

_____

_____

_____

_____

_____

_____

_____

_____

_____

_____

_____

_____

_____

_____

_____

_____

_____

_____

_____

_____

# NOTES:

# NOTES:

**Crestwood Public
Library District
4955 W. 135th Street
Crestwood, IL 60445**

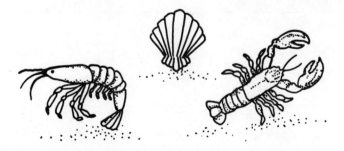